GREEK MYTHOLOGY

FOR BEGINNERS

GREEK MYTHOLOGY
FOR BEGINNERS

BY
JOE LEE

FOR BEGINNERS®

For Beginners LLC
155 Main Street, Suite 211
Danbury, CT 06810 USA
www.forbeginnersbooks.com

Text & Illustrations ©2013 Joe Lee

A For Beginners® Documentary Comic Book
Copyright © 2013

Cataloging-in-Publication information is available from the Library of Congress.

ISBN # 978-1-934389-83-6 Trade

Manufactured in the United States of America

For Beginners® and Beginners Documentary Comic Books® are published by For Beginners LLC.

First Edition

10 9 8 7 6 5 4 3 2 1

CONTENTS

Yes, the birth of Christ does figure into the antics of His cousins across the middle sea. In this section we will introduce the gods in all their lust and splendor. They will be presented in a chronological order of sorts from Chaos and the coupling of Gaea (Mother Earth) and Ouranos (Father Heaven) to the birth of Christ and the subsequent death of Pan.

1. CHAOS
The original condition, the undifferentiated mass from which all things are formed.

2. OURANOS AND GAEA
The first principals, heaven and earth, male and female, the parents of all that is to come.

3. EROS
The mighty and irresistible. Just try to go a round with this one.

4. THE TITANS, THE CHILDREN OF HEAVEN AND EARTH
- Oceanus: He dealt with—you guessed it—the ocean.
- Atlas: The guy who holds up the sky.
- Prometheus: The fire bringer, friend to humankind, and patron of Rockefeller Center.
- Cronos: Old Father Time himself and eater of his own children.
- The other slightly less titanic Titans.

5. THE TWELVE OLYMPIANS

- Zeus: Son of Cronos, lightning manipulator, and prodigious lover of women.

- Poseidon: God of the sea and brother of Zeus.

- Hades: God of the underworld and least-liked brother of Zeus; consequently, not very pleasant company.

- Hera: Wife of serial adulterer Zeus and, ironically, goddess of marriage.

- Hestia: Sister of Zeus and goddess of the all-important hearth. You've got to keep the home fires burning.

- Ares: Son of Zeus and Hera: god of war. It could have something to do with mom and pop's marriage.

- Athena: Daughter of Zeus and butt-kicking goddess of wisdom. Who says knowing something makes you a wimp?

- Apollo: Son of Zeus, god of music and healing and all-around pretty boy.

- Aphrodite: She was born in the sea and is never-to-be-denied goddess of love.

- Hermes: Son of Zeus, messenger of the gods and trickster. There is one in every crowd.

- Artemis: Daughter of Zeus and virginal goddess of the hunt who intends to keep it that way.

- Hephaestus: Son of Hera and blacksmith of the gods. It figures that the non–son of Zeus would end up being the blue-collar guy.

6. THE CAVALCADE OF OTHER DEITIES

- The Muses: The Sister Act of all sister acts, because there are no acts without them.

- The Fates: Even the other gods tremble at what these ladies do with thread.

- The Graces: And then there were three more ladies and these were lovely.

- Dionysus: The interloper from the East and god of wine and abandon.

- Demeter: Sister of Zeus, uber-important goddess of the harvest, and mother extraordinaire.

- Pan: The son of Hermes and Amalthea the goat (it does get lonely in the mountains even for a god) and god of all things nature and natural.

- And a host of minor and not-so-minor deities who hang the sun (Helios) and the moon (Selene) and handle everything from strife (Eris) to whoopee (Eros).

Wherein one blind raconteur and a collection of poets and playwrights become immortals of a different sort. Everybody likes a good story, and we will explore some those stories that entertained the ancients around the campfire a thousand years ago and still entertain and enlighten us today.

1. THE ALLEGORIES

- Pandora: She who cannot leave well enough alone, or the old, old version of *What's in the Box?*

- Eros and Psyche: Who do you love? Or I only have eyes for you.

- Orpheus and Eurydice: Love is blind or else…

- Pygmalion and Galatea: A guy's just got to love his work and sometimes you just can't leave it at the office.

- Narcissus and Echo: Hey, good lookin'. No, not you. I meant myself. Didn't I just say that?

- Daphne: Sometimes all a girl can do is make like a tree.

- Persephone: Yet another girl running from a god and the creation of seasonal affective disorder.

- Phaeton: Never drive the car without dad's permission!

- Midas: All that glitters is gold.

- Atalanta: Sometimes the race is won by those that cheat.

- Daedalus and Icarus: These wings are made for flyin', and that's just what they'll do until they reach too high an altitude.

2. THE HEROES

- Perseus: Bad hair days and sea monsters, no matter. It's all about saving the girl.

- Bellerophon: A horse is a horse of course, of course, until it sprouts wings.

- Theseus: Taking the bull by the horns and back again.
- Jason: A-sailing we will go, a-sailing we will go, and bring back a thro-o-o-ow rug for the temple floor.
- Oedipus: Every boy needs a mama to love, but not that way.
- Heracles: The man, the myth, the god. It takes a lot of labor, but you get there in the end.

3. THE EPICS OF HOMER

- The *Iliad*: Beauty will get the beast, or rather, best of us every time—all this and a large wooden equine.
- The *Odyssey:* Wherein you can get home again, but it might take a while.

PART III. A FUNNY THING HAPPENED ON THE WAY TO THE MODERN WORLD

And other reasons why all that has happened in the past still matters. These tales of gods and heroes live on in our hearts and minds, if not always in our memories.

1. ROME

You take a little here and you add a little there and pretty soon you have a reason for doing whatever you want to do.

2. THE RENAISSANCE

The old world made new! Oh, and is it pretty.

3. Neo-Classicism
The old world made better and so pure in form and reasoning.

4. Nietzsche
You can't keep a good, or maybe not-so-good, god down.

5. Freud
The old world informs us of everything right down to the dream you had last night. Sometimes a myth is just a myth—or not.

6. Popular Culture
- Books: As old as the gods and still in fashion.
- Comics: "It's a god! It's a man! No, it's a myth in spandex!"
- Movies: Or the world according to Ray Harryhausen (the first guy to release the kraken) and his progeny.

DEDICATION

TO MY NEPHEW, JACOB,
WHO KNOWS THESE STORIES

AND MY SON, BRANDON,
WHO IS ONE OF THEM.

INTRODUCTION

Would there be a Western civilization without the Greek myths? Would we be able to define our civilization and ourselves without some reference to the grand, glorious, violent, sexy, and venal doings of those denizens of Mount Olympus?

For those of you unclear where Mount Olympus is, here is some instruction into the mythology of our ancient forebears of the Greek peninsula, the islands of the Eastern Mediterranean, and Asia Minor. Those forbears migrated to the south across the mountains of Eastern Europe with their sheep and rudimentary skills at farming. And they came by sea with sleek-lined ships and nets and goods to trade. Those forbears founded the cities of Athens, the seat of learning and sophisticated culture, and Sparta, with its almost mad adherence to discipline and the crafts of war. Those forebears created a world of sophistication, philosophy, and just plain "Sophia" that still instructs us today.

So strap on Hermes's winged sandals, saddle up Pegasus, or grab the nearest Harpy (remember to keep your eyes closed) and come along for the ride of your life. Let us think in terms of the Sphinx's famous riddle: "What walks on four legs in the morning, two at noontime, and three in the evening?" Let us fly to that world that is as old as Chaos and as fresh the psychological complex you just developed—the ancient and refreshingly new Greek myths!

Greek mythology, as a belief and a system of literature both written and oral, has arguably been second to only the Bible as the greatest driving cultural force for the descendants of those ancient civilizations that sprouted and grew around the Eastern Mediterranean Sea. In *Greek Mythology For Beginners*, I will present the pantheon—that immortal collection of rogues and heroes, misfits and tyrants—and the stories about these deities and their rude, raucous, sometimes raunchy, and deeply moving dealings with mortals. I will also describe their undying influence on our thought and culture, how each age from Rome to Shakespeare to Freud down to our own Marvel Comics and NASA have been enlightened, informed, and been inspired by these wonderful tales.

READY OR NOT —
HERE WE COME.

PART I.

THE GODS THEMSELVES, FROM CHAOS TO CHRISTMAS

1. Chaos

In the beginning—because from the Bible to Steven Hawking we humans have always pondered the origin of our universe and endlessly and often poetically theorize about it—was Chaos. Chaos was the dark and roiling stuff, or "non-stuff," that represents the original condition. It was the undifferentiated mass from which all things are formed. The fusion of all the elements. The potential from which all arises. The singularity. But Chaos is also the opening of that original condition, the splitting asunder of that crowded and pregnant nothingness. The Big Bang, if you will.

Chaos did breach, and from that cosmic gate came first Tartarus—the lightless depths of the universe that lie below and precede Hades— and Erebus, the darkness from which all darkness descends, the primeval shadow that blots out even the thinnest flicker of flame. And from Erebus in yet another grand and exquisite parthenogenetic display came Day—for we will ever beg for the darkness to become light. Then Erebus continued by impregnating Day (assuredly a feminine attribute of nature, and at this point we can naught but assume Erebus represents the masculine side of the coin) and fathered the Sky.

So it began, according to that early chronicler, Hesiod, in his great poetic work *Theogony* written some 800 years after the time of Homer. Hesiod was not only a poet, but like our own Wendell Berry, a farmer, and his poem is much more than just a riotous epic of the origin of our own little piece of the cosmos. It is very much a religious work, and as we delve even deeper into these divine and dirty tales, it is always important to remember that these were not fairy stories to entertain and sometimes enlighten, but they are the stuff of human belief. The Greeks' very foundation of spiritual interaction with the world they found themselves in. They worshipped, prayed, and sacrificed to these gods. In their ancient equivalents of foxholes, they found comfort in invoking their names and begged their indulgence in times of distress.

2. OURANOS AND GAEA

Concurrent with the split in Chaos and preceding the twinned darknesses, another player pushed through into the brand spanking new realm of existence. Thus began Gaea the earth, our own dear original mother and mother of all the varied and wondrous creatures and all the elements, mountain, forest, stream, and sea, that make up physical existence as we know it. And she was mother to Ouranos, aka Uranus, the sky. And in true masculine fashion, Ouranos overwhelmed and subjugated his mother, the great feminine principal and principle, to his own bidding, coupled with her and gave birth to the first race of divinities—the Titans.

Of course, and so early in our travels, one can not fail to notice that the deities are not only forces of nature but also beings that seem to engage in the same activities we mere mortals do. They have sex. They give birth. They fight, make up, or bear eternal grudges. Are they "people" or are they "natural states?" The only answer that one can give is that they are two things in one. Let the mystery of the human mind do its typical job of allowing us to hold opposite and mutually exclusive thoughts and views firmly in place without causing our head to explode.

One might also notice that within the space of several pages two different origins of the Sky have been given: Erebus and Day are the parents of Sky and Gaea gives birth to the Sky, Ouranos, without benefit of a sire. There in the dim and murky reaches wherein our universe was born things get a bit confused, and as these stories were not written down until they had been told and retold for thousands of years, they certainly vary with the teller. Like the ancient Hebrews, things that are "irrefutable truth" on one page then become quite another "irrefutable truth" several pages on. Just read our Bible's Genesis Chapters 1 and 2 and try to resolve exactly when humans were created—was it before or after the animals? Best to "judge not."

Gaea, our mama, our soil, the solid ground beneath our feet is often represented by the creatures that are most firmly in contact with her—snakes. One sees the survival of her cult in the statues of her acolytes handling those long and subtle

WE WERE SACRED BEFORE WE TURNED INTO THE ENEMY.

reptiles that have engendered so much interest and fear through the ages. In ancient Crete, an island some 200 or so miles south of Athens in the Mediterranean Sea, the Minoan civilization seemed to value the power of this connection and created many representations of snake priestesses, or possibly goddesses in their own right, using snakes in their worship. Humans' seemingly universal aversion to snakes would appear to be some sort of rejection of this most primordial deity, but as we shall see, Gaea's direct offspring became some of the fiercest enemies of the future Olympians.

The history of our own little planet truly begins with Gaea and her son/consort Ouranos having their babies, and what babies those Titans turn out to be! Before we move too quickly past those oldest of times, we must speak of that greatest motivational energy in the universe.

3. Eros

Eros also found its way out through that terrible rending of Chaos at the beginning of time. Eros was not some overfed toddler armed with a toy bow and nonlethal arrows; no, that Eros would come much later and be overwhelmed by the tantalizing Aphrodite. This Eros, the original Eros, was a force of nature, a force that neither god nor man could stand against. At one time or another all creation could find itself in the passion of its irresistible embrace. This was not a "face that launched a thousand ships," but the force directed within the soul that could gaze upon that face and lead nations into war and devastation and the unreason that justifies such endeavors. This Eros seems not to have been personified but remained ever the energy that could set to motion all the doings both great and small that occurred outside the basics of eating, drinking, and breathing. No wonder that in terror of such power humans would try to domesticate it with diapers and silver wings.

4. The Titans, the Children of Heaven and Earth

OLD MAN RIVER, INDEED!

OCEANUS. One of the first offspring of Ouranos and Gaea was Oceanus. We have earth and sky, so we had better fill in the rest of this world project with a little water. Oceanus is the great circling stream that encloses the landmass of the world and the source of all the rivers that flow through it. Not much is said of Oceanus other than that he is personified as "he," not only by the ending of his name but by his marriage to his sister Tethys and the fathering of the Oceanids, those nymphs who inhabited this great world river. Of course, we must remember that according to ancient Greek cosmology, the realm of Oceanus was also the place from which the sun, moon, and stars ascended and made their clockwork descent and the vast watery plate upon which Gaea floated. Sometimes just being there is quite enough.

ATLAS. This Titan we remember not so much for his importance
in the pantheon but for the punishment inflicted
upon him. He was a grandchild of Ouranos and
Gaea, son of their children Iapetus and Clymene, and
brother to the uber-important Titan, Prometheus. Atlas, of
course, is the Titan with the big shoulders and a job to match. In
one telling he ran afoul of Zeus, who was at the time solidifying his
power against his forbears, and Atlas took the side of his siblings and
cousins. And it is never a good thing to choose the losing side. In
another version of the story, he has been demoted to the position of
an earthly king with a penchant for gardening (the gardens at the very
end of the earth—the Hesperides), and in his fabled garden grows a
tree with the most wonderful fruit—golden apples (a fruit which might
keep the doctor away but certainly cannot keep gods and humans
out of trouble). Perseus, fresh from giving Medusa a much-too-close
haircut has heard tell of this delectable delicacy and would like to
sample a piece. "No!" says Atlas, at which point Perseus gives
him a glimpse of the Gorgon's still petrifying eyes, and in an
instant, Atlas shrugs his mighty shoulders up from earth
to the very edge of the sky. Growing larger still he
becomes the mountain that becomes the
heaven's rooted support.

I LIGHT UP YOUR LIFE...

PROMETHEUS. If you were to know any of the Titans it would probably be Prometheus. He was a darling of the Romantic poets, a favored metaphor of Enlightenment intellectuals, an arousing model of art deco sculptors. He is also credited in some accounts with the creation of humans, so he will always rank high with members of that particular species. The story goes that Prometheus and his brother Epimetheus, as two Titans who had sided with Zeus in his war with those earlier gods (yes, there will be war), were given the pleasant task of forming all the creations that would inhabit the lonely earth. Prometheus delegated his tasks to his brother, who set out with gusto. Gathering, sculpting, and attributing all the strengths to all the various animals was a work of creative joy for Epimetheus until he got to his last creation—humans. By that time he had used all the wings and feathers, fur and claws, and strength and endurance on all the other creatures. Humans were left hairless, vulnerable, and terribly unappealing. Prometheus, whose name, after all, means "foresight," was not surprised at his brother's failure and stepped in to finish the job. He raised humans upright on two feet to walk like the gods, gave them cunning and intelligence to think like the gods, and—what else could he gift these pathetic creatures with to give them an advantage? Fire most certainly would do the trick! And Prometheus promptly stole flame from the heavens and taught humanity not only its many uses but also how to make it. Naughty god!

10

Zeus was none too pleased at this state of affairs and wanted some sort of reckoning with the Titan. Our dear Prometheus, even in this precarious position with El Supremo, ever the trickster (and always the trickster must trick even when putting himself deeper and deeper in the doo-doo), devised a contest, a taste test of sorts, and none other than Zeus would be the judge. Prometheus took a cow and separated it into its constituent parts—hide, bones, meat, fat, and stomach. Then he wrapped the fat around the bones and covered it with the cowhide. *Voila!* A cow is born, or, at least, the shape of a cow is born. Prometheus then stuffed the juicy meat inside the stomach creating an early Greek version of haggis. Now it was time for Zeus to select the cut of his choice. No brainer. Zeus chose the plump cowhide with what seemed to be its nutritious and delicious contents and Prometheus presented the "loser" to the lowly humans. With increasing anger and disgust, Zeus unwrapped his prize and even if he could have taken a bite of the oozing gelatinous mess, his fury with Prometheus would have spoiled his dinner. The Titan feasted with the recipients of his largesse and burped his praise to the god-all father.

As if this was not enough to completely sever any smidgeon of goodwill Zeus might have remaining for Prometheus, Prometheus still could not help himself. He had a secret, and it was one that could potentially rend the heavens. A beautiful Nereid named Thetis had caught both the eye of Zeus and his brother Poseidon. Neither god was particularly subtle in their wooing, but neither was quick about consummating either. Mr. Foreseeing knew exactly the problem that the lords of sea and sky were intuiting—it was fated that whoever had a son by Thetis would be destroyed by that son. Rather than spoil the result and settle the unease of the gods, Prometheus thought a little knowledge might provide a whole heap of insurance, but his calculations were wrong. Zeus hauled him to mountains of the Caucasus and had him chained to a rock. Every day a vulture dispatched by you-know-who picked away at Prometheus's liver. Every night the injured organ would grow back. How our great benefactor suffered. Just when it seemed it would never end, along came Heracles, he of the bulging muscles and a not inconsiderable intelligence. He bargained with Prometheus to break his chains in exchange for a little immortality-mortality switch-up with Chiron, the centaur. It seems somewhere along the way Prometheus had lost his immortality and Chiron, suffering with incredible pain, had gained the deathless condition without the reward. In the end, the horseman could die in peace and the Titan could live free again and forever. Prometheus unbound!

CRONOS. Old Father Time himself was young once and like so many young sons, the enemy of his father. Why couldn't they just get along? Ouranos was a jealous and tyrannical ruler of the heavens and the earth, his wife. Whenever she gave birth, Ouranos buried the child deep in the belly of his mother—from womb to tomb was a very short trip, and to those Titans, a familiar locale. But Cronos would have none of it. He with the help of his mother clawed his way back to the light and on his emergence, his rebirth, was presented with a sickle—a potent tool from Mother Earth and a terrible weapon in the hands of a Titan. Armed and ready for a scrape, he attacked his old man. A war in heaven! Time proved the victor, and the price rung from his father was great. Ouranos's blood dripped from the skies and spawned monsters when it fertilized the fecund soil below. Giants burst up from the vicious sperm and they were joined by their sisters, the Erinyes, the Furies, those shrieking avengers of familial crime. But Cronos's revenge was not complete; he would make his cruel father sire no more and with a slice of his blade severed Ouranos's testicles from his body and flung them into the churning sea below. They sank to the bottom not quite empty, for as they leaked, the action of sea and semen birthed she of the half-shell, Aphrodite, goddess of love. Now Cronos would rule the sky and set the world ticking to his time. He took his sister Rhea as his wife and they, the happy couple, provided new and divine offspring. But Cronos learned nothing if he didn't learn that sons are ready to depose their fathers, and his very own children could be the authors of the end of his tale, so he took those children, Hestia, Demeter, Hera, Hades, and Poseidon, one by one as they were born and placed the tiny bundles in his gaping maw and swallowed them whole. His belly filled with an entire generation of gods. However, Rhea disguised a stone in swaddling clothes to fool Cronos out of the meal of their final child, Zeus, and she hid the newborn on the isle of Crete and he was suckled

13

and raised to maturity by the goat Amalthea. Long years passed but a mother's love is longer, and after much coaxing, Cronos was willing to disgorge his bellied brood—first the stone and then child after child. Zeus, for he was the last sibling and the only one not to suffer gastronomic incarceration, had grown to virile godhood.

He returned to his parents' home and roused his siblings to rebellion. Cronos raised his own siblings, the Titans, and the monsters that earth, their mother, had birthed in grief through the hard years—the Cyclops with their one great eye and nasty appetites, and the huge Hecatoncheires, man-beasts with multiple heads and a hundred arms. The war was devastating as it ranged across the world—a war of flood, storm, lightning, as well as clashing armies armed with everything from tree trunks to swords. But ten years in the younger generation clamied victory and threw the vanquished Titans and their horrible allies in chains down into the deepest abyss of Tartarus. The reign of Cronos was at an end—but don't kid yourself time was not defeated and still it rules today.

THE LESSER TITANS. Yes, some are just slightly less titanic than others, but they still deserve to be mentioned. Ouranos and Gaea had twelve children in all, six of each sex. We have talked about a few of them, but among the others is Hyperion, who is often mistaken for or simply just renamed Helios, the god of the sun. Erebus is worth a mention, because where would we be without him? But a lot of the real action occurred during the reign of Cronos and Rhea. Night gave birth to *Doom* and *Death*, but let's not get too gloomy, because she also mothered *Sleep* and all the little *Dreams*. Night's procreation didn't just stop there, for she continued with *Gaiety* and his twin and opposite, *Misery*. She followed those kiddos with the never-forgotten and always-blamed *Fates*, who we shall discuss later. Night never seemed to sleep, because she proceeded to bring from her dark recesses into the light of creation god/attribute after god/attribute: *Nemesis, Sorrow, Hunger, Murder, Disease, Battle, Quarrels, Old Age*, and *Incontinence* to name just a few more of her many offspring. In fact, she was mother to an entire litter of troubles—maybe we could put them in a box to keep them away from the world and give that box to an impetuous young woman for safe keeping, but more about that later. Night, of course, was not the only deity involved in this great birth project. To different parents were born Iris the rainbow, Selene the moon, the white-tressed Graiae *sisters,* and the snake-tressed Gorgons. Those early days were a busy time of Titans growing the work of creation and populating the world with all the beauties, wonders, and horrors with which it is still populated. We may have to go to Tartarus to visit a Titan, but their children visit us daily.

5. The Twelve Olympians

The Olympians were so called because they took over the real estate at the summit of Mount Olympus, the highest mountain in the chain of mountains that separate Greece from Macedonia. The five sibling Olympians, Zeus, Poseidon, Hades, Hera, and Hestia, conscripted the Cyclops to build them beautiful and spacious palaces with views of the world, at least the parts they cared about—let Odin and Thor and their bunch take care of the frozen North. Comfortable accommodations complete, the gods and goddesses set about making little gods and goddesses to fill the empty rooms. Soon Ares, Athena, Apollo, Hermes, Artemis, and Hephaestus were underfoot and growing to the immaturity that served as adulthood among the divine. Aphrodite was a special case in that she wasn't sibling or child, but she was invited in. Eventually, a few other gods joined them, chief among them their sister Demeter, the sad and fruitful mother, and those very special demigods who were invited to reside with the originals, but they could never quite call themselves Olympians and always retained a state of exalted "boarder."

ZEUS. We have seen how Zeus was spirited away by his anxious mother to the isle of Crete from a father bent on having him as dinner, and there in a cave on Mount Ida he was wet-nursed and cared for by the she-goat Amalthea with the very capable assistance of the nymphs, Adrasteia and Ida. When Amalthea died Zeus willed one of her horns to the nymphs, a horn that always spilled with plenty of the abundance that life has to offer, the cornucopia. After he brought his father low and restored his brothers and sisters to a full life, rather than the purgatory of gastric juices and undigested food they found themselves swimming in, Zeus set about solidifying his power. The world lay before the brothers; the sisters were relegated to important but (in terms of temporal power) less meaty roles, and they needed to divide it. Lots were drawn: Poseidon won the sea, Hades the dour underworld of the dead, and Zeus the realm of sky and the solid world that lay beneath it. He took the thunderbolt as his scepter and weapon and never hesitated to hurl it earthward in anger or triumph. Zeus also took as his bride his comely sister Hera, but no vow of fidelity could hold him in her arms. He wandered the world in various guises from swan to shower of gold and spread his seed as often and as expediently as his fancy took him. He did, indeed, father belligerent Ares with his wife but took to bed many other goddesses to become the progenitor of Apollo, Athena, Artemis, and Hermes, as well as many other minor deities. Among the mortals, he managed to give rise to an entire army of heroes—Heracles and Perseus being chief among them. Zeus was never one to deny the charms of his own gender and fell in love with the beautiful young man Ganymede; trading some particularly fine horses to his father brought him to Olympus as his cupbearer. Zeus, capricious as he might seem, was honored as the great "father-protector" of god and man. He was all-seeing and all-knowing, a wellspring of knowledge and divination. He was filled with generous compassion when it suited him and righteous and vindictive cruelty when angered. He was the great judge and final arbiter of the divine and the mundane. He was the supreme being, and he wasn't afraid to let anyone know about it.

POSEIDON. As you might remember, Poseidon, brother of Zeus, took part in the biggest lottery ever—the one that divvied out heaven, earth, and afterlife. Poseidon was the lucky winner of the sea. Poseidon was considered pretty much on par in power with his brother in the sky. The sea was the most important and efficient means for travel and commerce. If one wanted to get somewhere in a jiffy, he or she better get a boat. Of course, Poseidon didn't always see his realm as coequal with Zeus, and he was at times a sea-green jealous monster. He even went so far as to capture Zeus and tie him up, but rescue came in the form of Briareus, who, with his hundred arms flexing for action, came up from way down below to free the "King of the Gods." Curses! Poseidon had his other disputes, but with each clash he always ended up all wet. Acceptance can be such a hard thing for a god—let alone the rest of us. He seems to have let that divine temper flare on numerous occasions, because the nicknamed "earth-shaker" kept the ancients hopping and dodging bricks many a time. Armed with his trusty trident, a device he never left home without, he would pound on the solid earth and set it to rocking and rolling. He would also raise the waves and wipe out not only sailing vessels but also entire cities and villages by the sea. Best to keep the sea god happy. So sailors always made a sacrifice and blessed their good fortune when Poseidon would breach the waves mounted on the glistening back of a dolphin, followed by his retinue of shell- and seaweed-bedecked mermaids and mermen, to protect the fortunate sailors.

HADES. If a vote were taken for least popular god, Hades would certainly be the winner. Without a doubt his chip in the great heavenly lottery was the one that nobody wanted. But it was one of those jobs that someone had to do. Though ruling the afterlife and underworld was a grim job, it was a job with which every human mortal would at some point become familiar. However, Hades was also the god of wealth, because all those precious substances like gold and gems had their origins down below and it took someone with a shovel and the goodwill of the king of death to get them. As foreboding as Hades certainly was, we must never fall into the false belief that he was evil. The ancient Greeks may have feared his realm and been frightened of his judgments, but he was never considered a devilish presence. He was always considered tough but fair. Of course, some of the servants of his realm took on even more frightening aspects. Charon the boatman's task was to row the deceased across the river Styx and would leave some poor ghost wandering forever if their dead eyes were not closed with a coin payment for him. Cerberus the three-headed dog (or as many as fifty heads in some tellings) would snarl and snap at the very gates of this dismal land to keep all the earth's departed from departing this realm. Hades, as the underworld itself came to be called, consisted of two main sections: the Plain of Asphodel, where most of the dead resided in a grey world of unending ennui, and the Islands of the Blest, Elysium, where only the very best people lived in eternal bliss. Punishment seems not to have been a general requirement for evildoers but was meted out for those special cases that had offended the gods in specific ways. Sisyphus seems to have been chief among these famous malefactors. Sisyphus was a king and a very sly customer known for his tricky ways. He once tricked Death (Thanatos, not Hades) into shackles and only released him with the pledge to skedaddle. Upon Sisyphus's death, Thanatos arrived to bring him to Hades. Upon arrival he pled to Hades to return home, where his spouse had dishonored his mortal remains by leaving them unburied. Hades, the fair, consented and back to life Sisyphus went to reunite with his mourning wife, thereby cheating death again. He lived a long time and when he could no longer avoid or wile his way out of the inevitable, he marched downstairs again to his unending punishment. He was charged to roll a huge stone up a steeply rising hill. Upon reaching the top, he would lose his straining grip only to have the stone swiftly roll to the bottom again. There he must start the procedure over only to have the same results. And day after dreary day on into eternity, Sisyphus must roll the stone. Best not to fool the gods.

HOW COME WHAT GOES UP MUST COME DOWN? GRAVITY HASN'T BEEN DISCOVERED YET!

Tantalus, yet another king with a streak of the conman in his soul, managed to steal ambrosia from the tables of the gods themselves. It was so delicious that, after sampling some himself, he shared it with some other friends. Tantalus knew he was headed for a heap of trouble, so he quickly arranged a big soiree for the Olympians where his own son became part of the feast (who knows what the kid did to become the main entrée). The gods chowed down and soon discovered that they had just dined on Tantalus Junior. Tantalus was immediately dispatched to the deepest depths of Tartarus to stand forever in a pool of water, water that tickled his chin whiskers but would instantly recede when he dipped his mouth to drink it. Over his head grew a fruit tree constantly in fruit, but when Tantalus reached to pluck a ripe one, the bough would snap back out of his reach. He was constantly tantalized and never fulfilled. Hades was tough but just.

HERA. Beautiful Hera. Daughter of Cronos and Rhea and sister of Zeus, who eventually became so much more to the great lightning-tosser. She seems not to have taken an active role in the great war of the Titans but had her allegiance to the winning side. After all, if you spent the first part of your life floating in your papa's stomach muck, you would probably side with your brothers and sisters, too. Separated from the turmoil of battle, she didn't get to know her family in the light of day, and while strolling the byways outside the city of Argos one day, she was espied by none other than her lusty brother Zeus. Zeus promptly transformed himself into that seemingly silly, but oh-so-crafty of birds, the cuckoo. A terrible storm suddenly burst and torrents of rain not only seductively drenched the winsome Hera, but also drove the poor bird to ground. Sympathies aroused, Hera plucked the little bird from the mud and warmed it to her breast. Zeus was charmed, to say the least, and instantly assumed his majestic shape and promptly proposed to Hera. Happily ever after? Not exactly. Hera, goddess of marriage, patron of the home, suffered with a serial philanderer of a husband and a disturbed and disputatious home. She is also the goddess of fertility and is often depicted presenting a ripe pomegranate in her hand. Many times the would-be mother prayed for her fecund indulgence. Her animal totem was the cow that calves easily and has milk for more babies than her own. Hera was fond of peacocks, as well, but for a special reason. Hera, that lover of uddered livestock, chanced upon Zeus paying a great deal of attention to a surprisingly beautiful heifer—the heifer was indeed the nymph Io concealed in bovine form.

WHAT YOU LOOKIN' AT ?

Hera sweetly requested that Zeus make a gift of the cow to her. The divine Don Juan could do naught but assent or refuse and be found out. Hera took the heifer by the ear and led it to her herd to be guarded by Argus her watchman. And Argus was a most excellent watchman as he had not two, but rather one hundred eyes in his head and only two would ever shut at a time in sleep. Zeus was terribly perplexed, so he sought the counsel of Hermes, messenger and trickster. Hermes would not disappoint. Out to the fields he flew armed only with his little syrinx (panpipe) and his abundant wit. "Hello," he called to the faithful guard. "Bet you could use a little company." And with that he proceeds to talk, play a little lullaby or two on the syrinx, talk a bit more, play another soothing little tune, tell another story, play a smidgeon more music, and, lo and behold, all of Argus's eyes closed in sleep. As quick as a bee-sting Hermes took his sharp little sword, separated the watchman's noggin from his body, and made off with Io. Another job well done for the wing-footed one.

Hera was bereft, bothered, and beside herself with anger, but before seeking revenge she plucked the eyes of Argus and "bedazzled" the tail of the nearest peacock with them. A touch of beauty before dispatching a swarm of gadflies to devil poor Io's hide. The cow sped to the shore in hopes of outrunning the biting menaces but they followed all the way across the Bosporus (cow-ford), down the coast of Anatolia and Palestine, cow-paddled the Red Sea, and got all the way to Egypt. At last, Hera relented and Io happily resumed her proper shape. As the protector goddess of mothers, Hera had children of her own. None was as important as her son Hephaestus, one of the twelve principle Olympians. Some report that he was the son of Zeus, but the better story is that after Zeus birthed Athena right out of his own noggin, Hera was thrown into a jealous rage and by her will alone conceived, brought to term, and gave birth to the little godling without the help of god or man. Now that's a mother!

HESTIA. Hestia was guardian of the fire, patron goddess of the hearth, and center of the home. The other gods swaggered, bullied and battled their way in the heavens, Bronze Age Greeks (who weren't really Greeks at all but rather Athenians, Spartans, Corinthians, etc., who just happened to share a common language and the rudiments of a culture) battled across the dust of the earth and the splash of sea, but Hestia remained the good, solid core of life keeping the home fires burning. The gift of Prometheus would ever be her sacred altar, although altars in every city were erected to this homebody goddess. Few stories have accrued to flesh out her personality. She seems to have at some point or other in her career been pursued by both her brother Poseidon and her nephew Apollo (even in the world of the incestuous gods, this does still rate some of the *yuck* factor). Hestia refused both and preferred to remain a virgin, untouched by masculine hands. Not even the gods can touch a flame but must simply honor its power and importance. Thank you, Hestia, for always being home.

ARES. The *bad boy* of the Olympus crew, Ares seemed to have been disliked by everyone, including his parents Zeus and Hera. He strutted about in his bronze armor clashing and bashing and making the most discordant music; the music of war. Nobody worshipped him and no one did him honor. But he caused trouble on both the battlefield and in day-to-day life. Ares was a bully and, like so many other bullies, he had to be tolerated because of his family ties. And also like many other bullies, he would show the cowardice underlying his bravado if he was injured or bested in battle. He often appeared on the field of combat with his little darlings Phobos (whose name translates as fear), Deimos (fright), his not-so-sweet sister Eris (discord), and her baby boy Strife. He was also attended by his symbolic beasts—the vulture (no surprise there) and the dog (dogs of war, sure, but what a sad master for man's best friend). With a retinue like this one must ask, "Where's the love?" And, of course, the love, Aphrodite, was sometimes to be found in the armored embrace of Ares. Love is blind, indeed! This act of betrayal—Aphrodite was the wife of the war god's brother, or stepbrother, Hephaestus—did not go unnoticed, and that meekest of gods and husband of Ms. Love had his revenge.

He, the builder of the Olympians, fashioned a net with an ingenious mechanism that when tripped would capture the offending prey. Hephaestus strategically concealed his trap under the canopies and hidden in the soft bed linens where he suspected the illicit lovers would conduct their next tryst. And he was correct. During the act of consummation, the trigger was sprung and into the air the naughty pair was captured and caged for all to see and scorn. Shame had its desired effect and Aphrodite came home to her clever but perhaps uninspiring husband. Ares, despite wishing revenge, was afraid of Hephaestus's important status and slunk home with tail tucked firmly between his legs. Although this was not Ares's finest moment, he does seemed to have faired much better as the defendant in the first recorded murder trial. Ares had a lovely daughter, so different than her other siblings, named Alcippe. Poseidon's son Halirrhothius lusted after Alcippe. Halirrhothius stalked, was spurned, and then in anger, raped Alcippe. Ares, in a true display of fatherly heroism, killed the vile son of the sea. Poseidon was furious and sought revenge, but cooler heads prevailed and a trial was held on the Areopagus (Ares's Hill) in Athens. Testimony was heard, evidence was examined, and the force of the words of the real victim, Alcippe, carried the day. For once, Ares was vindicated. Even the bad boy can sometimes do good.

26

ATHENA. Finally, we get to a little wisdom in this rash and rowdy crew. Before we get to wise Athena we do have a little ugly backstory to deal with. Hera was not Zeus's first wife. He was married first to Metis the goddess of wise counsel, but having heard a prophecy that the children of Metis would be smarter than their father and could take over the whole show from their old man, Zeus made like his pop and promptly swallowed Metis. He also had the keen awareness that sometimes the contents of one's stomach can come back up in dire consequence, so he digested Metis and absorbed her knowledge and wisdom. Sometime after this feast of "brain food," possibly nine months later, Zeus started experiencing some knockout headaches. He, however, did not crave pickles and ice cream, but Hermes, seeing him in such distress figured out what was happening. He quickly summoned Hephaestus, bidding him to arrive with his mighty hammer in hand. Hermes had Hephaestus take one good swing at Zeus's paining bean and *crack!* The supreme god's head split like a melon. Out of the fissure sprang Athena in full armor and shouting to beat the band. Athena was possessed with the drive and determination of her dad but was also filled to brimming with the wisdom of her fully digested sort-of-mother. She was always sought for her sensible and patient problem-solving abilities. It is certainly with simple good sense that the industrious, hard-working, and hard-thinking Athenians would choose her as their patron and name the city

27

after her. She was also designated as the patron of craftsmen and working women. The Acropolis, that magnificent hill crowned with its world wonder of a temple in the center of Athens, was her special place, but this was not indisputably so. Poseidon also claimed possession of the Acropolis and had to be dissuaded from pursuing his claim with a well-reasoned argument. Athena was smart enough to not only engage the full swaggering, testosterone pumped boys of Olympus but to be able to back up her words of wisdom with a strong and efficient sword arm. She also had the good sense never to engage in any amorous pursuits with these divine man-children and remained one with the sisterhood of virgin goddesses. Athena did, however, have favorites among mortal men. Although she never consummated any fleshly behaviors with them, she certainly displayed her love in other ways. Fond of the young bucko Perseus, she let him in on the secret of the Gorgon's eyes and armed him with a mirrored shield. In gratitude Perseus awarded her with Medusa's severed head to adorn her breastplate, the invulnerable Aegis. No other favorite gifted her with such an outstanding token, but many a hero sang the praises of her aid in times of trouble. Gray-eyed Pallas Athena accompanied by her familiar owl was ever beloved by mortal men.

ATHENA THAT'S WHO!

APOLLO. Apollo was so much more than a pretty face, but when you're as pretty as Apollo, that is easy to overlook. He began life as the favored child of Zeus and Hera, the rare occasion when they seemed to be able to agree on something. He was fed ambrosia and nectar from birth by Themis, a daughter of Prometheus and Gaea and the goddess of oaths and bonds. With such exquisite care he achieved full manhood in four days—they do grow up so fast. Apollo became the god of light (not the sun but light, and what it means to the soul, in general), music, and prophecy. He even went by the additional moniker Phoebus, which translates to "the bright." But before we get too carried away with this wonder child, it is important to remember that there is a variant version of his parentage and the troubles it caused. No, Hera was not the mother of Apollo in this telling, but rather it was Leto, a Titaness known for her sweet and gentle ways. Artemis was her firstborn by Zeus, which instantly incurred the wrath of Hera. They fled from island to island with Hera in hot pursuit, finally arriving on Delos where the lad was born. It wasn't long before everyone was in love with shining little Apollo. But Apollo wasn't exactly in love with everyone. In the version with Leto as his mother Apollo was mighty mad at a particular serpent that Hera had dispatched to torment his mom. The snake in question was appropriately named Python. Apollo tracked down the offending reptile on Delos, pinned it with an arrow from his silver bow, and,

29

using the sturdy sword that Hephaestus had crafted for him, whacked the fork-tongued head clean off. One small mistake: He killed the serpent right by the steaming fissure in the earth where the oracle sat and made her prophetic pronouncements. Bright boy or not, Apollo was in some pretty deep doo-doo. Atonement is good for the soul even if that soul resides in a god, and Apollo was placed into servitude with King Admetus as penance for his crime. Apollo created the Pythian Games to honor his dead enemy, and it made everything good. Even better, because of his new connection to the place of the oracle, he became the patron of all the seers who then also took the title of "pythoness" in remembrance of Apollo and his stunning retribution.

Apollo was also the god of music and he was quite enamored with his reputation as the celestial strummer. With lyre in hand he could soothe even the most tone deaf of beasts and where sweet notes would not suffice, jealousy would take over—when you are considered the best you may not want to share the stage. Orpheus he may have accepted for his extraordinary gifts as a musician (although Apollo's son Aristaeus wasn't quite so tolerant), but Pan (or Marsyas the satyr in a variant) would not make beautiful music with our bright and brilliant boy god, as we shall see in the tale of Midas. It may come as a surprise that a fellow this beautiful and who so often treated others with graciousness, was not always considered quite the catch. He wooed Princess Coronis after seeing her bathe her lovely feet in the cool water of a lake only to have her later spurn him for Ischys, the Arcadian. Apollo sent a crow, a blazingly white bird at the time, to spy on the lovers and when the crow reported back to the god too late to stop Coronis and Ischys from making whoopee, Apollo blasted the crow's feathers black. The human lovers did not fare quite as well as the bird. Artemis, in a pique about the treatment of her brother, let fly with her arrows. Coronis fell to the earth dead, pregnant with Apollo's child. Apollo was able to play midwife in time to save the baby from the funeral pyre. He named the boy Asclepius and gifted him with the power of healing. Asclepius grew up to become not only a much-loved and revered demigod, but also the patron of medicine.

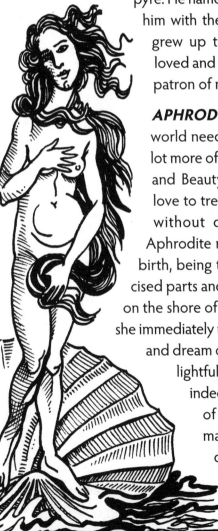

APHRODITE. She is certainly what the world needs now and could have used a lot more of then, but this goddess of Love and Beauty was not the first version of love to tread the celestial stage. She was without doubt, the most attractive. Aphrodite may not have had an inspiring birth, being the byproduct of Cronos's excised parts and sea foam, but upon stepping on the shore of Paphos on the isle of Cypress, she immediately made everyone forget her past and dream of their own future—and a delightful dream it was. Aphrodite was indeed a vision, and it was this vision of beauty that every god and man prayed to attain. She was indeed an attainable vision for many of them; though she was wed to the lame and terribly ugly Hephaestus, that didn't stop her from making other males' fondest dreams come true. Aphrodite's long and torrid affair with Ares, which resulted in the "netted" couple literally being hoisted into the air for ridicule, also resulted in three children: the not so delightful daddy's boys Phobos and Deimos and a girl who took after her mother, Harmonia. She also conceived children with Poseidon, Dionysus, and Hermes, among other gods. Her child with Hermes is noteworthy because the kid was truly a chip off both of the old blocks. Hermaphroditus began life as a male, and an exquisitely beautiful one, no less. He was observed bathing by the nymph Salmacis, and she was instantly and irredeemably smitten. Hermaphroditus was having none of the comely young maiden and sent her packing to finish his wash-up. But Salmacis was not one to give up so easily. What seduction couldn't get her she thought maybe prayer would, so she prayed that if the boy would not possess her in the old fashioned way then she would want their bodies to be forever joined—one body, two sexes. Her prayers were answered and Hermaphroditus became the guy with something extra, who had a little more difficulty deciding which restroom to use. But as we stated earlier you didn't just have to be immortal to sample our Lady Love's favors.

LET ME SLIP INTO SOMETHING A LITTLE MORE COMFORTABLE— C'MON WHAT DID YOU EXPECT THE GODDESS OF LOVE TO SAY?

Anchises was a shepherd tending his flocks away on Mount Ida. He was also a Trojan—not even a Greek to boot. Aphrodite couldn't fail to notice the good-looking fellow as he protected his lambs from the wolves; he could find no protection for himself from the wiles of a goddess. Bliss ensued and nine months later little Aeneas was born —who became the star of his own Roman epic the *Aeneid*. Aphrodite swore Anchises to absolute secrecy as to the identity of baby's mother. The shepherd agreed "mum" was the word. But Anchises was a human after all. He had "made it" with the goddess of love and that is a powerful incentive to brag. And brag he did until even the ears of Zeus rang with the story. When Zeus gets mad you want to be in a sturdy, grounded structure, not a mountainside pasture. *Zap!* went the thunderbolts, and the only thing that saved Anchises from becoming roast mutton was that fair Aphrodite managed to deflect some of the blow; he ended up with just a bum leg instead of a funeral pyre. Sweet Aphrodite. Everybody loved her but she was always a little separate from all the others. She wasn't really a sister or an aunt. But no matter how "other" she might be, she was of central importance to everything. Without love there would be no religion, no culture, and no people. Some things are so impor-tant that if they didn't come riding the waves on a clamshell, we had better just invent them.

HERMES. We recognize him even today with his winged sandals, his golden staff, and his winged soup bowl cap. Hermes the rascal, the trickster, the wit of Greek mythology moves through the tales with a grace and humor few other gods achieve. Hermes was the son of Zeus and the nymph Maia, a daughter of the Titan Atlas. Only hours after his arrival he started his mischief. Outside his cave birthplace in the mountains of Arcadia, the cattle of Apollo grazed. Hermes took an instant liking to these magnificent bovines and decided he wanted them for himself. He fashioned himself sandals that looked like they belonged to a large man as opposed to a newborn and were turned around as if the wearer were walking in the opposite direction. Out to the pasture stomping his absurdly shod feet he had the cattle shuffle off backwards. When Apollo came to look over his herds he was shocked to see them gone and with Hermes's little sandal trick he couldn't quite figure out the direction in which to follow them. He stood scratching his shining brow in utter confusion until an old fellow lounging on the hillside, who had witnessed the entire pro-ceedings squealed on the toddling little jokester. Apollo hied himself to the cave in a mighty uproar. But our little hero knew how to gentle the raging beast. He had divested the old tortoise that lived at the mouth of the grotto of his shell, took gut provided by one of Apollo's cattle, and strung it to create the first lyre. As the angry god approached, Hermes sat sweetly strumming. When could a god of music stay mad when a bouncing beaming boy pre-sented him with such a lovely gift? Hermes's career was off. Zeus invited the lad to Olympus and took great pride in his boy. Hermes also seemed to be tolerated, if not liked, by Hera even after that in-cident with her prize cow and her watchman. His body could move swift as his mind. In no time, before the other immortals had Hermes shuttling from Olympus to Earth and back again. Hephaestus fashioned him a pair of winged sandals, the talaria, to accelerate his already blinding speeds. Topped with his jaunty winged cap, Hermes moved even faster than one of Zeus's thunderbolts. Apollo forgave Hermes's joyful transgressions and gifted him with a golden staff as the symbol of his status as messenger to the gods.

Once, while racing about his beloved Arcadia, Hermes chanced on two serpents locked in biting, thrashing combat. Never a fan of violence, Hermes cast his rod between the wresting pair and instantly they peacefully and protectively entwined about the gold shaft. Thus the caduceus was born, which to this day still symbolizes healing (although it does get mixed up with Asclepius's serpent adorned staff, which is the badge of medicine). Some accounts say that the serpents in question were not braided together in a vicious death match, but rather caught in the act of reptile love when Hermes inserted his staff betwixt the lovers and, *voila*, a phallic symbol is born.

Hermes was also considered the male symbol of fertility. Columns of an erect masculine shape often topped with a representation of the god's smiling head, called "herms," were placed in gardens and along roadways to invoke good fortune in the ways of love. Needless to say, Hermes sired many children. He was patron of commerce and thieves, travelers, gymnastics, and anything that required a quick wit and a supple body. It may come as a surprise that our happy trickster also had a gravely serious function. Hermes was the psychopomp; the guide of the dead. He

35

would appear at the time of a person's demise, touch them with his staff, and lead them to the underworld. But in the end, who could be a more congenial guide than our laughing, delightful Hermes? At the very least the journey to the afterlife might be made more pleasant with his company.

ARTEMIS. Artemis was the mistress of the beasts. Running wild with the creatures of the wood she was spotted by many the lonely hunter but never trapped in the arms of these erstwhile lovers. Artemis remained a virgin. Yet a dramatic and perplexing statue in Ephesus shows Artemis with many, many breasts. She seemed to be prepared to suckle the whole world. Times change and the old fertility goddess becomes our chaste huntress. Artemis was the sister of Apollo and as he was often (and mistakenly) identified with the sun, she was considered the moon, Selene. Although Selene is often seen as a separate deity, Artemis certainly fits the profile of the moon—cool, remote, and untouchable. Our goddess of the woods was happiest in her leafy environs far from the intrigues and caprices of her fellow Olympians. Surrounded by her companion nymphs and dryads she hunted only the older beasts, for she was also protector of the young. Yet, when her chaste enjoyments were interrupted she was no longer gentle. A hunter, Actaeon, came across Artemis cavorting with her familiars in a stream while tromping through the forest in search of suitable game. Actaeon looked on from beyond the shrubbery as the naked goddess was groomed and petted by the equally nude nymphs. What man could resist such a charming and alluring sight? Actaeon's hounds stirred and disturbed by the interruption, Artemis spied the spy. The goddess's mood changed in an instant, and throwing her hand out in anger toward Actaeon, she flung drops of water at his hot and lusty face. Instantly, the hair of his head and face moved downward to cover his entire body, his arms and legs stretched, hands and feet hardened to hooves, and a beautiful rack of antlers pushed upward from his skull— the hunter had become the prey. Actaeon had become a stag and as quickly as this change occurred his dogs transformed from friends to foes and set upon their former master. The chase was brief and the hapless hunter was torn to shreds by his own dear hounds.

Artemis could be a hard case and this quality is exemplified in her as Hecate, yet another identity. Hecate was an ancient Near Eastern earth goddess whose biography became hopelessly entangled with our huntress. She was at once a patron of fertility and, what became to the Greeks a more important aspect of her character, a witch. As a witch she is celebrated and feared by many a Hellenic writer. The fear won out and she became associated with the underworld and the dead. So Artemis was a tripartite goddess and a figure in three realms: Selene the moon in the heavens, Artemis the huntress of the earth, and Hecate deep in the underworld. One could argue that she was always present in some form, but be careful when you look at her.

HEPHAESTUS. While the other gods might be lying about on overstuffed golden couches and gorging on nectar and ambrosia, someone had to get things done. That someone was the always-industrious Hephaestus. Ugly, lame in the legs, and indelicate as the most earthbound blacksmith, Hephaestus's craftsmanship is legend. Homer tells us he was the son of Zeus and Hera but Hesiod disagrees and counters with his story of Hera's jealousy producing a son on her very own. Everyone agrees that fatherless or not, Hephaestus was lame from the very beginning of life and his handicap was both a blessing and a curse. Hera was deeply discouraged after her efforts and in characteristically godlike fashion dropped the newborn right down the mountain of Olympus, but Hephaestus was rescued and nurtured by the Nereids, Thetis and Eurynome. Ever the yoyo, Hephaestus popped back to Olympus after dusting himself off and it wasn't long before he was displaying his vast usefulness to the other gods by tending to the forge. Hephaestus was the maker, the artificer, the craftsman. He was the laboring god, the god whose hands weren't bloodied by ridiculous squabbles but dirtied by his honest work. Whenever a god needed something special—a helmet to grant invisibility, an impenetrable shield, a breastplate to display the severed head of a Gorgon—it was our thick-shouldered god of the swinging hammer that got the job done.

I DID IT MY WAY!

After an argument with Zeus, Hephaestus took another unscheduled, unscenic trip down Mount Olympus and once again was given succor by Thetis, who by now was a married woman and a mother. It was as a mother she begged a favor of the smith-god. Thetis had a son, a warlike child for whom she had sought every protection. She knew that he would spend his life in battle and, in addition to her efforts, he could use more insurance. Could Hephaestus pound sheets of bronze to clothe his body and greaves to secure his legs? The grateful god reinstalled at his forge atop Olympus and tailored for the young Achilles a suit of armor more protective than his own mother's arms. None was happier than Hephaestus when doing his work. No grateful marriage to the goddess of love Aphrodite (still a good, albeit, faithless catch) could replace the joy of creating, the magic of transforming, and the satisfaction of manufacturing by muscle and sweat the wondrous artifacts that filled the halls of Olympus and glinted close on the bodies of the gods. All in a day's work of a god.

IDLE HANDS ARE THE GODS' PLAYTHINGS.

Gods, gods, and more gods. The Titans and the twelve Olympians aren't all. Ancient Greece was bursting at the seams with gods—and that wasn't easy because a *chiton* was a seamless garment. Beside the major deities, almost every aspect of existence and every facet of human emotion had an accompanying power. Night, day, dawn, sun, moon, anger, happiness, and olives had their patron gods. Aristaeus, a son of Apollo, was the god of olive cultivation and beekeeping (more about him later in the sad tale of Orpheus). If something new was invented or something unknown discovered, a god came hastening along to take credit or possession of it. So many gods, so little space. What follows are some of the major non-Olympians (though many did call Mount Olympus home).

THE MUSES. Would it be even possible to write this if it weren't for those lovely sisters, the Muses? There were nine of them in number and all of them were the daughters of Zeus and Mnemosyne (Memory). Although each of them represented a specific attribute, none of them were distinguishable from the others, but that was okay because they always appeared together. They became more important in Greek life as religion became more formalized and culture grew to be the central pillar in the temple of Greek thought. Calliope was the muse of epic poetry. Clio was the muse of history. Erato was the muse of lyric poetry. Euterpe was the muse of the flute. Terpsichore was the muse of the dance. Thalia was the muse of comedy. Melpomene was the muse of tragedy. Polyhymnia was the muse of mime. Urania was the muse of astronomy. Although there are not any adventures associated with these goddesses, no stories to be told around the firelight, no anecdotes to relate about their origins, we, or at least, the ancients, would have been hard pressed to tell any of the wondrous stories found herein without the aid of these Muses. Sometimes passing the gifts of culture is the greatest adventure of all.

THE FATES. Hesiod may have been the first to actually name these three sisters, but they may be older than the other gods (even though some argue they are daughters of Zeus and Themis or even bridal attendants at their marriage). And they are surely in their quiet way more important than their fellow deities because in their hands lay the individual stories of both gods and men. The beginnings, the middles, and the ends slid through their ageless fingers. The Moirae sisters, the Fates, were also known as the *Klothes,* the spinners of the thread of life. Clotho spun the thread from the spool, Lachesis pulled the thread into its shape, and Atropos, most feared of all, snipped the thread to end it all. No one knew where they kept their residence, possibly nowhere and everywhere, and no one knew what appeal could be made effectively to them. Often they were exhorted or even cursed, but imperturbably they went about their work. May your thread be long and golden and the scissors sharp.

THE GRACES. Who among the gods has had more artists set their depictions in stone and paint? Who among the gods has been more sought after, more fantasized over, or longer remembered than those three lovelies, the Graces? Who among us would not treasure more time spent with Thalia, the flowering of good cheer and prosperity; Euphrosyne, joy; and Aglaia, radiant splendor? These children of Zeus and the daughter of Oceanus, Eurynome, were ever together, ever dancing, the inseparable triumvirate of what the good earthly life can bring. They appear sometimes as the attendants of Aphrodite but most often appear on their very own, without any other function than to be their own happy selves. Only one, Aglaia, ever appears to have done something that didn't include the others and that was to wed the unhappily married Hephaestus, who had suffered the slings and arrows of an adulterous spouse. Is it any wonder that our Graces were always invited to every wedding of both god and man? The Graces are probably the only ancient deities to be honored by Christianity, albeit in a slightly transformed version. St. Paul in 1 Corinthians 13:13 says that almost all earthly things will pass away but only three shall abide forever: *faith, hope,* and *love.* The three theological virtues are the Christian variations of the sisters. Paul, ever the urbane and sophisticated intellectual, could see the value in these principles of goodness and that even the old pagans could sometimes hit on the truth. Everybody can use a little grace and so the Graces dance on and according to Paul will keep spiraling those steps forever.

MAMA!
UH,
DADA?

DIONYSUS. Now it's time to party! The god of "*laissez les bons temps rouler!*" as they say in New Orleans—"let the good times roll!"—has arrived. But, as with most good times, it took a while to actually get there. And there were those who didn't see those times as all that good. Dionysus was by most reports the son of Zeus and Semele. A variant tale has him as the son of Zeus and Persephone and it took no time before the displeased Hera sicced the Titans on him. They chowed down leaving only the lad's heart, which Athena retrieved. Zeus swallowed it and with the deposit of some very potent seed, it wasn't long before sweet Semele gave birth to the little Dionysus—the "twice-born." Zeus then zapped the Titans to ash and used the ash to form the first humans. Always with the ashes to ashes. While still in the womb Dionysus was already the declared enemy of Hera. Hera was clever and tried an indirect assault on the unsuspecting expectant mother. In disguise, she befriended and then disturbed the happiness of Semele with questions about the identity of the father. At last, Hera had her way and the befuddled Semele demanded that Zeus truly reveal himself to his pregnant lover. Sorrowfully Zeus unveiled his full glory and Semele burned to a crisp. Hermes, quick as a whip, snatched the embryonic god from the cinders and ash and sewed him into Zeus's thigh. Shortly thereafter the supreme god was delivered of a precocious 8 ½ pound tumor. A god was born! Champagne was not uncorked and happiness did not ensue for our young Dionysus, because Hera was not yet satisfied in her revenge. She chased the poor young fellow from pillar to post and right out of old Greece. He had a collection of various foster parents who were afflicted with an assortment of madness and ill fortune. One after another these surrogates came to a bad end. All the way to Asia Dionysus was hounded, but travel, even with dogs of disaster nipping at your heels, still broadens the mind, and the young bravo learned much about the world—more than most of the other gods combined. After years in the East he slowly worked his way back to Greece and he did not come alone. Dionysus came home with a retinue of devoted followers and a purpose. He would not be denied his birthright, and he had a magic elixir to melt even the most calloused and reluctant heart. Dionysus had become the god of wine, the god of ecstasy, and the god of wild orgiastic abandon. He conquered the land with an army of satyrs, nymphs, centaurs, and creatures that possessed human characteristics but still had the distinct features of the animal world. Wherever this band of joyous troops traversed they left not wreck and ruin but cultivated vines; ammunition to spread the gospel to human brethren. And the cult grew and prospered with tilted cups and mouths painted purple from the sweet and bitter flow of the blood of the

THIS ONE'S FOR YOU.

grape. Even Hera had to at last and reluctantly give in to this all conquering new god and his happy sacrament. But not all of Dionysus's
rites were family friendly affairs. His human followers, decidedly
women followers, were called *maenads*—mad women. They
weren't given this title because of wonderful hijinks, but because
when in their self-induced frenzies, they went truly and terribly mad.
They often danced in scraps of animal skins around a fur-draped
pole crowned with the image of their darling god, and woe to the
man who was caught in the environs of the orgy. As the Greek play-
wright Euripides relates in his tragedy *The Bacchae,* the unfortunate
and terribly willful Pentheus has Dionysus glam him up as one of the
girls just so he can attend the celebration. Poor Pentheus ends up
as a specie of "pulled- pork" sandwich once his ruse is discovered.
Boys do not get in the way of these girls that just want to have fun.
Dionysus may have had his 24-hour rolling party, but wine has to
come from somewhere, and Dionysus was also the god of cultivation—it all starts with a seed. Cultivation leads inevitably to civilization and you can't have civilization without laws. So, Dionysus with
his long curled and oiled beard, crown of grapevines, purple robe
and leopard stole, and scepter, (the *thyrsus,* a staff wrapped in
grape and ivy vines and topped with a pine-cone; a decidedly phallic object), went sowing his seeds of ecstasy and reaping the harvest
of civil society. Dionysus, "the god of the two doors," indeed.

DEMETER. Older than Zeus, but as new as the
fresh buds on the wheat was Demeter. She was
the goddess of the fruiting and fruitful earth,
planting, and the joys of a full harvest. Her breasts like twin cornu-
copias forever spilling their
bounty on the fertile earth.
Demeter was the goddess of
the ever-present blessings of
reality. Zeus was the god of remote and distant dreamy
skies. Which deity was truly
more important? Deme-
ter was the daughter

of Cronos and Rhea, sister of Zeus and Poseidon, and greatly desired by those gods of sky and sea. She spurned Poseidon who had assumed the shape of a stallion flecked and jeweled with sea-foam, and his hooves proved to be the winner in the race with her small feet. She gave birth to Arion the horse-man from this unwanted union. Zeus charged at her as a bull and once again the violated Demeter delivered a child, a daughter named Kore, better remembered as Persephone. Persephone was truly the apple of her mother's eye and the flower of her heart. She loved and doted on the beautiful girl, and when Persephone went missing, that heart was torn from Demeter's chest. Around the world the goddess wandered in her grief and the earth grew colder as she lost hope. Despair plunged the earth into cold, bleak winter; an icy grip that seemed it would become the lasting condition of the world. But miracles happen and Persephone was returned to her mother—where had she been these long dreary months? Ah, there's the tale and more to tell, but patience… Enjoy the spring and Demeter's joy to hold her warm daughter to her breast again. From then on the earth turned in its seasons and winter became spring, summer falls to autumn's harvest, and then the sad winter again filled with the hope of spring. Demeter, older and possibly more important, or at least more attuned to humanity, was celebrated around Greece but especially at Eleusis. Twice each year the Eleusinian Mysteries were consecrated with personal enactments of the goddess's quest for her daughter.

We still celebrate our own watered and half-remembered rites to Demeter when we turn our cheeks to the breath of warm spring air and thank our *Mother Nature*.

PAN. His name meant *all*. He represented no particular moral value or immoral failing. He was man and beast. Even the most sophisticated Athenians could be counted as his devotees. He was universal and personal. He was all. As with so many of the divines, Pan's parentage is in some question. Just exactly who was father and mother to this creature—the upper body of a human, albeit one with the brutish features of the genus *Capra*, and the lower body of a goat. One source has him descending from the conjugation of Hermes and Amalthea, Zeus's horned and hairy "nanny." It would make sense in that Pan possessed Hermes's merry and life-loving personality and the headgear and "rear-gear" of Amalthea. But in so many ways, the goat-hoofed god seems to have preceded into existence his presumed parents. He might have forever wandered the woods of Arcady, and beyond, with his panpipes in hand, protecting the flocks, chasing nymphs, and frightening the unwary stranger. Some of the earliest uses of art appear to paint his portrait in carbon and ochre dancing across the walls of European caves. And that is pretty old!

Pan always lived up to the name of the keratinous protrusions on his brow—his soul was as horned as his head. Always the teenager, he was on the prowl for a plump young lady to join him in his song and step of eternal laughing and earthy creation. Many a nymph, damsel, and dryad succumbed to his barbaric charms, but our dear Pan is more famous for the ones that got away. Syrinx, a beautiful and most charming nymph, could not keep from charming our not-so-beautiful goat-horned deity. He advanced and she rejected—over and over they danced the tango of non-consummation. But persistent Pan gave chase and light feet floated while hooves dug in, and just when it seemed that the god-in-rut would catch his retreating prey at the edge of a burbling creek, Syrinx's sister nymphs stepped in to relieve and end the race. They transformed Syrinx into a stand of reeds at the water's margin. Bereft, Pan fell to his hairy knees and wept without consolation until a passing breeze blew gently across the reeds' open mouths and out issued the most delicious sound. Seven of the stalks he carefully cut and with beeswax and grass bound them as he and Syrinx never would be. He began to play the most delightful and some-times melancholy reels across his invention, his panpipe, his syrinx.

Many others escaped Pan's musky advances, Echo chief among them—I'm sure you'll hear that again, but some happily and blissfully lost the battle and joined him in the making of Chaucer's "two-backed beast." Children are reported as a result. Some say the jolly pot-bellied drunk Silenus was his son and left his father's side for the slightly more gregarious Dionysus. Others seem to have scrabbled up the mountainside and lived their lives in the happy company of wind and blue-sky and cool glade. Pan did have his cult and fond religious followers all over Greece, but strange it might seem

49

that Athens, the city of all cities of the Greco world then and now, was the center of this rude and rustic god's worship. There was a very good reason: Pan was truly the savior of Athens and he did it not in the mythopoeic past but in historical times. Herodotus, the father of history, writes that before the Battle of Marathon the runner Philippides was sent out to enlist the aid of the recalcitrant Spartans in what would be the decisive engagement in Greece's great war with the invading Persians. After the Spartans refused their timely participation, the dejected Philippides trotted back to the embattled Athenians, and as he ran, he realized that his were not the only steps ringing against the stony mountain path; Pan was his erstwhile companion. Pan, noting his startled gaze, asked the young messenger a pointed question: "As I have always loved Athens, why has it not loved me in return? Why after all the times I have offered your city aid, never have you reciprocated by building a temple to my honor? Is a little appreciation too much to ask?" Philippides promised the god that if he would once again show them favor, the wrongs of the past would be righted forever. Pan was on the job.

The next day, as hoplite wrestled with eastern "immortals," and things were looking bad for the home team, Pan arrived and one look of his gnarled old "billy" visage sent the Persians back to their ships. Pan had lived up to the word that oftentimes described the startling sight of this goat god in human eyes—*panic* routed the invader that day at Marathon. And when the Athenians returned to the victory celebration at home, minus poor Philippides who died of exhaustion after making a 26-mile run, to tell Athens of their boys' success, they promptly built a temple to dear Pan in a cave on the Acropolis somewhere beneath Athena's Parthenon. Pan also figures in another historical account, a somber one. During the reign of the Roman Emperor Tiberius (CE 14-37) a sailor related to the historian Plutarch found that as the ship he was crewing on rounded the island of Paxi, all on board heard a terrible crying and lamentation coming inland from the beach. At last a voice called to the ship with these sad instructions, "Tell them the great god Pan is dead." So the Roman Popeye reported to Plutarch and Plutarch reported to the world. Did Pan die? Well, we do know at almost this exact time another powerful yet loving and peaceful god was being born in Bethlehem. The reputed death of Pan corresponds to the birth of Jesus Christ. Did Pan die? Did he perhaps cover his body in a new skin and green leaves and move to Neverland? Or return to visit the wee animals of bucolic England at the turn of the 20th century? Or maybe appear in the pine barrens of New Jersey as the "Jersey Devil?" Did Pan die?

GODS AND MORE GODS. Thus far we've discussed quite a few gods, but there are a lot more gods where they came from. Greeks were great synthesizers and inventors and always open to adding a few more gods. Like the proverbial clown car, you open the door and out they tumble. In brief, here are a few more:

Adonis—Sometimes a god and sometimes not, but always the pinnacle of male beauty. Variably the hidden child of incest beloved by Aphrodite and an adapted Middle Eastern god representing the fruitful year.

Aeolus—The lord of the winds. Zeus had bottled the winds up in a cave for Aeolus to let out when a breeze or big blow was needed.

Antaeus—A son of Poseidon and Gaea who was fabled for his strength but only when his feet were in direct contact with his mother, the earth. Talk about keeping your feet on the ground. Heracles did the rough and tumble with him.

Asclepius—He's been mentioned before. The son of Apollo and god of healing, but he is one of those that only achieved god status after his time on earth. Death was good to him. Snakes are sacred to him as a healer because they shed their skins and are forever renewed. That is why the snake appears on his and, by tradition, on all doctors' staffs.

Ate—Was she or wasn't she a goddess, or even a personification of a condition? Ate is that condition where all moral strictures are thrown off in blind pursuit of one's desire. It happens in love, it happens in war. Ate happens.

Attis—Another sojourner from the East, Attis is a representative of the "dying and rebirthing" vegetative gods. He castrated himself in grief and madness, was hung on a tree (or his spirit passed into the tree), and was eventually returned to earth.

Boreas—The god of the North wind. He carried off a princess of Athens and became very important to the Athenians thereafter.

Charon—The boatman of the dead. He ferried the newly arrived deceased across the river Styx to the afterlife proper, but only if the dead had been supplied with a coin, an *obol*, in the mouth. Without the moolah you were left to haunt the shores forever.

I'M TEACHIN' HORSE-SENSE!

Chiron—The centaur, and if the ancients had a patron of teachers, he would have been it. Some traditions have him as a son of Cronos. Unlike the other centaurs, Chiron was cultured, artistic, and wise. He was mentor to both gods and men. Heracles accidentally wounded him in the knee with an arrow that had been dipped in the hydra's blood, which would have been fatal to any mortal, but Chiron was immortal. Zeus figured out an arrangement where Chiron would surrender his immortality to Prometheus and be able to go peacefully and painlessly to his death.

Eos—The goddess of the dawn. Homer seemed much enamored of her "rosy fingers."

Eris—the daughter of the early elemental god, Night, and the absolute embodiment of strife. A faithful companion of Ares and always present at any conflict, she was definitely one goddess to avoid.

The Gorgons—These monsters are goddesses!? Yes, they were direct descendants of Gaea and the sea. They were also sisters of the hideous Graiae sisters, who we shall meet again in the tale of Perseus. Medusa became a monster because she had the misfortune of making love to Poseidon in a temple devoted to Athena. Athena was mad and decided to give poor and, up to that point, beautiful Medusa a new hairdo. Oh, Medusa, snakes are so you. The hapless, reptile-coifed Gorgon eventually gave birth to Poseidon's children through her neck after her head was severed, when Perseus gave her a very close haircut.

Harmony—The daughter of Aphrodite and Ares, she married Cadmus, the founder of Thebes. Her mom gave her a beautiful necklace made by Hephaestus as a wedding gift, which made the wearer instantly beautiful—and brought a whole lot of disharmony to Thebes. A gift that certainly kept on giving.

The Harpies—If the Gorgons can be goddesses so can the Harpies. These descendents of Gaea and Oceanus started out as wind spirits that liked to hijack unwary people and somewhere along the line became full-blown monsters. But they did have beautiful hair, according to Hesiod, and lovely bodies until you got to the waist and the scaly tail that comprised the rest of them. Aello and Ocypete, those dangerous fly-girls, appeared in several myths, most notably the tale of the Argonauts, and still frighten the modern imagination.

Helios—Also known as Hyperion, he was the god of the sun. He rocketed across the sky meridian everyday in his glowing chariot. From his vantage point he could keep an eye on all the doings on earth and report back to the proper authorities.

The Horae—Three sisters who were the embodiment of the seasons: spring, summer, and winter. No autumn for the ancient Greeks, so no leaves to rake.

Hypnos—The god of sleep, he was a benign character who soothed the tired to sleep with a touch of his wand. He had three sons who were very much dreamboys: **Morpheus**, who sent dreams of humans; **Phobetor**, who took care of dreams of animals;

and **Phantasos**, who was in charge of the dreams about inanimate objects. Hypnos is often depicted with one wing on the side of his head, maybe because we fly in our sleep but inadequately.

Iris—The goddess of the rainbow and the Harpies' better looking sister. She was also Hera's messenger since Hermes was often busy being Zeus's mailman and unavailable to tend to Hera's postal needs.

Nemesis—Another goddess who was also an abstract idea. She troubled men's and gods' minds. She was that vague feeling that you had left something undone, someone was after you, or they will eventually find out—and maybe they will.

Nike—Long before she became a shoe with a swoosh, Nike was the goddess of victory. The famous winged statue of her stands without head and arms but still triumphant in the Louvre and in many productions in CEO's offices and high school gymnasiums. After all these years Nike/victory is still pretty popular.

Pegasus—A horse is a horse, but Pegasus was so much more. He came flying out of Medusa's neck hole after she had her head whacked off. He was the son of Poseidon and the aforementioned snake-haired lady. This winged horse was the stuff of everyman's dreams. Pegasus still flies through our imaginations.

The Pleiades—The seven daughters of Atlas who were mercilessly pursued by Orion the hunter. First the gods turned them into doves to escape their relentless pursuer—not a great idea considering hunters' relationship to bows and arrows. The gods then transformed them into stars and placed them in the night sky. Eventually, Orion became a constellation as well—and the pursuit continues.

Priapus—A fertility god reputed to be the son of Aphrodite and Dionysus. Priapus is always depicted with a frighteningly large and erect phallus. Before the advent of Viagra, he was considered quite important, but if he visited for more than four hours you'd better call on Asclepius.

Proteus—An ancient sea god and servant of Poseidon, Proteus had the remarkable ability to change shape at will. He was also incredibly smart and packed to the gills with knowledge. Others liked to ask him questions, and when Proteus didn't like to answer—*presto*, you're talking to an octopus.

Selene—Goddess of the moon and often intertwined with Artemis. She, like Helios, was a charioteer with two silver horses in her charge as they pulled her across the night sky. She spied the beautiful Endymion asleep on a mountainside and contrived that he sleep forever so she could visit nightly and embrace his dreaming form. Selene still appears and Endymion snores on.

Silenus—Son of Pan. He was the patron god of slackers, and one of Dionysus's entourage. Balding, pot bellied, and disheveled to nakedness, his only attribute seems to have been jovial inebriation.

Thanatos—The god of death and brother of Hypnos. He was considered a kind god and one who could resolve the troubles of life, not the fearsome monster that pursues our thoughts today.

Tyche—The goddess of fortune. Not much is known about her other than that she was much called upon for luck as the other gods lost their status.

Zephyrus—The west wind, also known as Zephyr. He seems to have been better liked than his cavemate, Boreas, but the breeze from the west is always kinder than the icy blow from the north.

The nonhumans. The world of Greek mythology is populated with a lot more sentient creatures than the gods and the humans with whom they play puppetry. There is a whole host of almost human, almost divine, and "we're not quite sure" characters that need a little explanation.

Centaurs—Men to the waist and horse all the rest of the way, centaurs are the wild and wooly tramplers of the myths. They were bad enough sober, but they liked to drink and when they did, nobody was safe from their hooves, their lusts, and their tempers.

Dryads—Dryads were the nymphs of the forest. They were born when a tree seed sprouted and lived until that tree died.

Naiads—The nymphs of lakes, springs, and ponds.

Nereids—The nymphs of the sea and daughters of Nereus, a salty old sea deity.

Nymph—Any of a class of female elementals that were personifications of the natural world (e.g., dryads, nereids).

Oceanids—Another race of sea nymphs that happened to be daughters of the Titan, Oceanus.

Oreads—The nymphs of the

mountains.

Satyrs—Their appearance was a great deal like Pan's, with a human torso but the lower quarters of a goat and certain features of the head, pointed ears, flat nose, and horns that bore resemblance to an old billy's as well. They were raucous, perpetually horny, and unfailingly jovial. Satyrs were rustic but accomplished musicians and dancers—performance skills they put to use as members of Dionysus's retinue.

Sileni—A lot like satyrs but with the goat legs, ears, and tail by those of the horse. They are often associated with Silenus as well as being members of Dionysus's rollicking gang.

Sirens—They are sometimes described as having the bodies of birds but crowned with the beautiful faces of women. Some say they were daughters of one of the muses. One thing is for sure, you can look but you don't want to her them sing; their voices are a sweet and lulling narcotic that no one can resist. It was the last song a sailor heard as he crashed his ships on the rocks to get close to this most compelling of music.

Sphinx—An emigrant from Egypt, the sphinx transformed as a symbol of royalty into an alluring monster. She, because there don't seem to be any male sphinxes in the Greek myths, had the attractive face and torso of a woman, but the body of a lion and that lion's body would come to dreadful life when one failed to answer her riddle.

PART II.

THE STORIES THAT INFORM

Everybody likes a good story and Greek mythology is filled with some of the best and most influential stories ever read—and if you want to understand some of the thinking and idiosyncrasies of Western culture, these tales are invaluable. They are allegories and adventures that entertained the ancients around the campfire a thousand years ago and still entertain and enlighten us today. They tumbled around as part oral tradition for hundreds of years, undergoing who knows how many changes and modifications before they were finally written down. Some might actually have been the invention of a single individual; most were probably the work of hundreds of skilled and maybe not-so-skilled tellers and writers. And they have survived for this retelling.

1. The Allegories

These stories of foibles, loves, lusts, and on occasion glorious successes were more than yarns; they were very often the religious beliefs of the people that told them and their eager listeners. They informed and taught, perhaps not with a clear-cut moral, like an Aesop fable (yet another Greek tale teller), but in a more elusive and less blatant way. Some are very direct in their instruction, some are more mysterious, and all are meant to be pondered, enjoyed, and always to be told again.

PANDORA. The world was devoid of women. Men rutted about, joking, spitting, arguing, and bashing each other without benefit of a more refined opinion, a perhaps gentler or more subtle way of being. Zeus, angry with Prometheus's many unauthorized gifts to these savage testosterone-pumped humans, decided to send them a gift of equal measure—or a terrible curse depending on the teller. And Zeus called this gift woman. He had Hephaestus fashion her from clay and she was kissed with life. The rough hands of the god-smith created something delicate and even lovelier. The supreme god named her accordingly, or perhaps ironically, Pandora, "the gift to all." In keeping with her name the gods bestowed on her a dowry, which was meant never to be viewed or even known. In a magnificent golden, jewel encrusted casket the gods each placed an attribute. But these attributes were not to be wished on anyone. They were curses, calamities, and sins venal and mortal. They were the entire catalog of sorrows that could befall humanity. But the unsuspecting new woman was not just set on the surface of the earth without instruction; she was given one and only one command: Do not open this box that had been given to you for safekeeping. And, box in arms, she arrived at the home of Prometheus's brother, Epimetheus. Epimetheus was instantly smitten with the enchanting creature that greeted him on his doorstep. Pandora was equally charmed with the Titan. Love grew and in a ceremony never experienced on the earth's surface before, Pandora and Epimetheus were married. If only we could say they lived happily ever after. Sometime after their blissful joining Epimetheus was called away on some sort of antediluvian business and Pandora was left alone. Curiosity, that

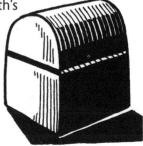

quality that has lead humanity to Olympian heights and the lowest depths of Hades, was in abundance in the soul of dear Pandora. She fretted, resolved, fretted, and resolved again and at last the strain was too great; she succumbed. Her little hands secured the box and placed it in the center of the floor close to the fire pit to better see what it contained.

Slowly, she opened the clasps that held it fast and then she forced the lid open. Like a scream of agony all the ills the world could ever know and even fathom came rushing out into the unprotected air, the innocent and unsuspecting realm of men. The casket opened and Pandora saw, experienced, wept with sorrow, and struggled to pull the lid down and trap these punishments back in the golden prison, but they had escaped to do their harm across the planet and in the souls of all they encountered. Pandora could save only one attribute; this was the only one that was slow to go and wished to linger with the young woman. Hope remained in the box and remains in the container of every human soul since the first woman. Our *everymother* let curiosity guide her hands and obedience leave her mind. Sounds a bit like another first woman I read about…

EROS AND PSYCHE. Aphrodite had a son, whose father might have been Zeus, and she named him Eros. Eros was the apple of her eye and the rich and newly ripened fruit of her soul. Eros was also the functionary in her ongoing quest to bring love to all corners of the world. He was armed with golden arrows that, when loosed from his golden bow, unerringly struck their target. And there they caused their wonderful and aching hurt, the wound of love. No god or human was immune from the power of these little shafts and no one could hide from Eros's aim. But Eros also had another weapon in his quiver. Lead arrows, arrows that when used on some unfortunate soul had that person finding their self out of love, bereft, and pushing away from what had once been their deepest desire. Love is powerful and not to be denied.

Psyche was a princess in a world populated with many, many princesses. Every city, town, and village had a princess, or two, or three. But Psyche was different than all the other princesses. She was the most beautiful princess, the most beautiful woman in the entire world encircled by Oceanus. No arrows were needed to make men desire her or women to fall under the spell of her beauty. Word of this rare gem reached the heavens and Aphrodite was not pleased. In fact, she was angry with this young and un-suspecting competitor. Acting impulsively on her jealousy, Aphrodite sent word to Psyche's father, the king, to lead his beautiful daughter up to the top of the mountain to be punished for her in-fraction, the grave infraction of being too pretty. Aphrodite then dispatched Eros to carry out the punishment on the unwitting beauty. Eros, as if pierced through the heart by one of his own arrows and indeed wounded to the core, took one look at Psyche and fell completely under the spell of her incredible looks. Instead of punishing her he took her in his arms and whisked her away to a palace high atop another mountain, a palace in architecture if not in furnishings. The cool marble halls were devoid of any of the accoutrements and furniture of other royal abodes. It was truly Spartan; only the necessities of quotidian life broke the expanse of the empty chambers. And beside the god, who Psyche could not see because he had rendered himself invisible to her sight and anonymous to her knowing, the princess seemed completely alone in the entire structure. But not alone because her every desire was intuited and unseen hands instantly fulfilled her wants and needs. It was a strange prison that enclosed Psyche and she would have died from the need for companionship, except that every night her captor cloaked in the impenetrable robe of darkness came to her and lay with her on her couch. They lay like lovers, the most ardent husband and wife, and through the hours of night they knew each other, sleeping very little. Every morning with the first hint of rosy fingers tickling up the belly of the sky Eros left the wedding bed for his work in the world.

Poor Psyche, who had been so used to the bustling, crowded world of her birth, spent the day with only the quiet touch of ghostly hands to keep her company. When Helios again made his descent from the heavens and the stars winked on to replace his glorious all-encompassing brightness with their charming and meager lights, Eros came home to his Psyche. They spent the next hours in unseeing bliss and then and always Eros departed with the dawn. Psyche occupied herself as best she could with her mountain views and internal dialog, but the night was when she truly came to life. But even in this nightlife, Psyche was thwarted and held captive to Eros's proviso that she was never to see him. His looks and identity must forever remain unknown. How Psyche suffered; she needed to gaze not just on her mysterious lover but on another human face.

The calendar rolled on, turning day to night, and Psyche's moments of complete happiness were sharply punctuated with the stark realities of her solitary confinement. At last one night her need to see overcame her pledge. She heard her love's gentle breath coming in the long slow measures of sleep and she put an ember to the candle at the bedside and the light sprang up. She held the candle up to at last see the face and shape of the man who had been her captor and now her dearest heart. Psyche saw Eros! She saw the beauty that equaled her own in face and form. Her joy leapt up as one hot drip of candle wax fell down, down to singe a tiny spot on Eros's soft chest. He instantly awakened and saw the startled eyes of Psyche plunging into his own. She had seen him! Psyche had seen his face and she knew! Faster than thought, Eros cursed his bride for being untrusting and as if scarred by one of his own lead arrows, his love turned to hate and he left her side vowing to never return.

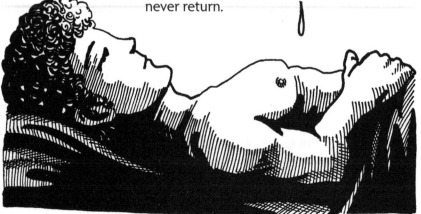

Psyche was truly alone. In morning light she made her way down the mountain, her sorrow adding an even greater burden on her descent. She was friendless, frightened, and hungry for some small understanding of her condition, but Aphrodite, who discovered the tale of her son in love and his gorgeous prisoner wife, was not about to end her feud with Psyche. The goddess of love hated the princess and hounded her with labors and tasks—Psyche was ordered to separate the tiniest grains of different plants that filled an entire storage chamber within the space of a day (Psyche was helped by pitying aunts); she must gather the golden fleece of fierce man-eating sheep (Psyche waited patiently and gathered it from the brambles and briars that groomed the savage rams as they went back and forth on the riverbank); she even had to plunge to the very depths of Hades on a seemingly impossible punishment decreed by Aphrodite. Psyche fulfilled each assignment with her own natural intelligence or with aid rendered to her and with kindness and compassion. As Psyche labored, Eros healed from his burn and with the sting gone, he was able to remember his own true love. He escaped the ministering chamber of Aphrodite's palace and searched for his dear Psyche. He found her and took her once again into his capturing arms but this time not to secure her in some remote incarceration but to bring her to Mount Olympus. Psyche was redeemed and rendered a goddess by Zeus himself and even Aphrodite had to at last accept her as daughter-in-law. Of course, Psyche never really left the earth but lives eternally here in the consciousness of every mortal. Without the beauty of Psyche embedded in our brains we would be dull and plodding creatures, not the curious and sometimes self-destructive humans that we have become.

ORPHEUS AND EURYDICE.

Orpheus was a singer, lyrist, and musician who, with a stroke of his fingers on silver strings, could bring the very stones to give up tears. Orpheus's voice was so sweet that not even jealous Apollo could envy him his talent. Orpheus, who it was said was son of a muse, inherited his talent and surpassed even his mother's ability to inspire. Orpheus was famed throughout Greece and his art was viewed in the sublime realm of perfection. He had sailed with Jason as one of the Argonauts, that crew of heroes that included even Heracles, and he had on several occasions been their savior. It never came at the expense of his brawn but rather it was with the use of his skills as a musician. The ship, the *Argo,* was driven aground and no amount of muscle applied to block and tackle could loose it from its berth, but Orpheus played and gently the sands gave up their grip and slowly pushed the beached vessel back to the lapping waves. When the sirens called their irresistible song to the hearty crew, Orpheus sang his song, drowning the narcotic lure of the bird maidens of the rocks and the *Argo* was saved from crashing at their taloned feet. The terrible clashing rocks were halted in their all-crushing squeeze by his song, and even the dragon that guarded the golden fleece could offer no resistance to his profound abilities.

Orpheus was the hero that quelled a thousand raging enemies, yet he could not quell the conquering assault of love. Orpheus fell in love with Eurydice. Eurydice was a dryad, a race of tree elementals, and in what forest Orpheus encountered her we do not know. But we do know with the first sight love took root and grew without stopping in the fertile earth of his heart. And Eurydice loved in equal measure. A wedding was announced and invitations issued to gods and men. The day arrived and the guests brought universal joy at this blessed union. It was universal joy except for Aristaeus, Apollo's son, who also wanted Eurydice for his wife. Even after the ceremony he schemed to be with Orpheus's new bride. Schemes failed so he attempted confrontation. He stalked his quarry, laid in wait, and when Eurydice presented herself he pounced filled with his raw animal lust. Eurydice ran, and her bare feet pounding against the earth summoned a snake, a viper. The reptile struck, fangs plunging into the young woman's ankle. In agony the dryad fell and before Orpheus could add his breath to hers her soul fled to that other land, the land below. Orpheus mourned, but his mourning would not stay his feet; to Hades he would go and bring his dear wife back. Days, weeks, months passed until at last he stumbled at the gate to the underworld. Armed only with his lyre and his voice, he reached the fetid entrance and stepped down. With every encounter—Cerberus the watchdog, Charon the ferryman—his voice subdued all obstacles until he gained Hades's throne. Eurydice sat with the lord of the dead and his wife, Persephone. Orpheus gasped and pleaded his case in song. Hades melted but not enough; the hard heart of justice still held solid. But

Persephone was moved so deeply by the sad tale of the lovers that she begged her husband to relent. What music couldn't do his wife could, and Hades at last agreed to let Eurydice return to the land of the living but on one unshakeable condition: She must walk quietly without making the slightest contact behind Orpheus and he must not glance backward to check on her progress. Orpheus must trust that Hades would keep his bargain and that Eurydice would indeed follow. Under pain of her returning forever to the dark halls of the underworld, he must keep his eyes forward until they stepped out of the darkness and into the world of light and life.

Without hesitation the couple agreed and immediately set forth on the journey upward. Through the plain of Asphodel they picked their way; melancholy souls blocked the path to inquire of the news from where they wished to return, but Orpheus turned them away and continued, and Eurydice followed. Through the tunnels and chambers, the labyrinth that confounded the reasoning of the most freedom-committed spirit, Orpheus led, and Eurydice silently matched step for step. Across the river Styx, Charon rowed the anxious Orpheus, and Eurydice silently sat behind. They passed Cerberus, his snapping jaws still gentled by the remembered strains of song; Orpheus rushed, his anticipation growing, and Eurydice glided as if her feet did not make contact with the floor. Orpheus's heart beat the drum of fear as he perceived the first faint glow of returning light—Is she behind? Has she been snatched back? He listened and hearing nothing, not the tiniest brush of foot on stone, robe against rough rock, he shook. Is Eurydice there? Has Hades played me for a fool? No! He tried to move forward to the growing illumination, but his feet were bound to the condition of his heart and they would not move. One quick glance. A movement of the head and eyes so slight as to be imperceptible that is all. His neck turned, his eyes shifted, and Eurydice came into his sight and as quick as her look of deepest love and eternal sorrow met his eyes, she departed as if she were merely smoke in wind.

Eurydice was gone. Forever gone. And Orpheus was alone. Alone he did the only thing he knew to do, he sang. The mountain trembled to hear the song of grief. Birds fell from the skies. The trees bent double. The stones poured streams of salt tears. Orpheus sang until he could sing no more and fell in exhaustion to the path. He slept the sleep of bitter dreams. As the singer slept, a band of maenads came rushing up the path, their reason expelled by the throes of savage ecstasy that inhabited them. They saw not the musician crumbled in the most abject sorrow the world had seen, but a man as a barrier to their progress. They dropped on him like vultures on a carcass, their hard nails and sharp teeth ripping into his arms and legs. In an instant the musician was reduced to shreds of meat. Only his head remained intact to testify that this carnage had been a man. The head they tossed into a stream. The shock of cold water awakened that last small spark and the head faintly returned to song. From the stream to the river and out to the great sea, at last the song was lost in the endless pound of waves. The gods placed the lyre of Orpheus among the stars to help all who look upward to remember the music and above all to trust the gods.

PYGMALION AND GALATEA.

Pygmalion was the king of Cypress, fabulously rich, impossibly handsome, and terribly unhappy. Pygmalion was unhappy because nothing satisfied his unexpressed desires; nothing fulfilled his well-hidden longings. Those desires and longings were not for women, Pygmalion would assert. Whatever it was that had happened in his past to build such a temple of disdain in his heart for the opposite sex, it had constructed a foundation that was seemingly earthquake-proof. The chambers of his heart were filled with blood but empty of love. However, Pygmalion did have a hobby. He lived to take chisel and mallet in his hands and face a block of cold marble. He would swing and tap, shaping the lifeless stone into the lifelike image of one of the gods. This pleased the sculptor and it also pleased the gods. One day surrounded by chips, flakes of marble and with the heavy stone dust floating through the air, Pygmalion became inspired. He would challenge himself to sculpt a softer and, some might say, more difficult substance, and he would not look to the gods for models. He would use every bit of his considerable talent to fashion a woman from ivory. She would be a woman whose beauty would be unrivaled by all the women of flesh and blood that he so despised.

Pygmalion searched every merchant vessel that hailed from the south, from Africa, and every caravan from the east, from Asia, for the largest, most flawless tusk that ever framed the trunk of an elephant. Finding at last the most exquisite ivory, Pygmalion set to work. He cut and sanded, slowly shaping the fragile substance. He slowed his labor to take in and appreciate every subtle change. And day by day, hour by hour, a woman emerged from what had been the living tooth of the giant pachyderm. After months of unflagging work, Pygmalion stood back to admire the skill of his hands and mind. There before him stood the most perfect, the most beautiful woman. As naked as Aphrodite emerging from the waves or Artemis from her bath, she stood. Pygmalion chose to name her Galatea.

Now named she seemed even more nude as she stood in the warm sunlight that fell across her on her pedestal. Pygmalion purchased the most delicious silks, the gaudiest brocades to drape her breathtaking form. She stood chastely, but still there was something profoundly wrong. She was not alive—and Pygmalion, after all the hours realizing Galatea's creation, had fallen irresistibly in love with the product of his work and ardent imagination. Pygmalion rushed to the temple of Aphrodite, made his offerings, and prayed as he had never prayed before for a miracle, a favor, some token from the goddess of love that he had in the past done honor by sculpting. Pygmalion wanted a woman, a woman to mirror the one of ivory that stood in his studio. Always bemused by humanity's feeble attempts at warding off her gifts and their loud declarations that she held no sway in their tiny lives, the goddess consented. Love will always win. And as he prayed before the altar of Aphrodite, he saw with his own eyes the flames leap upward three times. Without hesitation he rushed back to his workroom. Pygmalion rushed to his statue, the fruit of his labor and, as if in goodbye took her cool ivory hand in his; soon the woman of his dreams would arrive. The sunlight must have warmed the hand. He rubbed his hand up the perfectly formed arm only to discover that the parts of Galatea

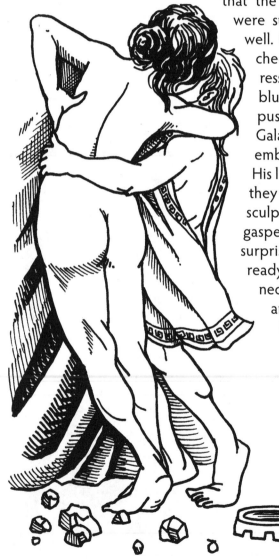

that the sun had not found were suffused with heat as well. His fingers found her cheek and under the caress of the tips that cheek blushed and then pushed into a smile. Galatea lived! Pygmalion embraced his creation. His lips found her lips and they kissed until both sculptor and sculpted gasped for breath. It is no surprise that these two already so intimately connected souls fell instantly and unreservedly in love. Somewhere in a palace on Mount Olympus a goddess smiled her gentle smile of victory.

NARCISSUS AND ECHO. Narcissus, the son of a nymph and a river (such couplings happened then), was a beautiful young man. Anyone who had the pleasure of gazing on his perfect face and form could not deny themselves the further pleasure of staring. Narcissus was quite taken with himself and not one to pay much attention to those lesser beings that could not equal his perfection. Echo was a pretty young nymph, but she wasn't *that* pretty, and she had the misfortune to tumble into love with Narcissus. Poor Echo followed the boy, calling sweetly to him. Narcissus ignored at best, insulted at the median, and behaved in a fashion not to be repeated at the worst. Echo still followed and called even more sweetly. But sweetness could not move the conceited pretty boy. Still Echo called, and called, and called. All her energy was put into the plea for some small recognition, some small token of affection. No, Narcissus was a wall unmoved, a deaf ear, a heart hard to the nymph's voice. Echo wasted away from unrequited love, but her voice remained, calling still. Aphrodite was enraged to witness pure and unadulterated love thwarted by such callous disregard. She would have a suitable revenge. She called Eros to her service and sent him with an arrow nocked in his bowstring to visit Narcissus. One straight golden missile pierced the formerly impregnable heart as Narcissus gazed at his own reflection in a still clear pool. Such love the world had never

known before as the fondness, deep and abiding, that Narcissus exhibited for himself. He could not tear his gaze away, not even to eat or sleep. Narcissus, as he had allowed Echo to do before him, wasted away with his eyes firmly gazing into his own reflected orbs. In the very spot where he faded into nonexistence, a small white flower sprang from the sod that was still marked with his indentation. We still call that flower the Narcissus as a remembrance of what pretty does. And Echo is still calling, calling.

DAPHNE. Daphne was a nymph, daughter of the river god Peneus, and she was a committed priestess of the Mother Earth. She like all the other priestesses of the cult had taken a vow of celibacy, and it was a vow she had no interest in breaking. Daphne's situation was complicated by the terrible curse of having been born with the gift of uncommon beauty. Her gift made her greatly desired by many suitors. Her curse was to be pursued by those suitors. She wanted nothing to do with any of them and wanted just to be left alone to worship with the other priestesses in their women-only forest services. The suitors had all been mortal until they were joined by none other than Apollo: beautiful, charming, the shining prize of Olympus.

The situation for Apollo was complicated—a beautiful nymph who wanted nothing to do with any male and an entire battalion of rivals to deal with, maybe not divine competitors but some very capable and worthy mortals who were after marriage and not just a roll in the shrubbery. Apollo took care of one, Leucippus, who had the bright idea of getting close to his intended by dressing himself as one of the mother goddess's female aspirants. He with a bronze razor, no doubt, gave himself the closest shave possible, but there were certain body parts he would certainly not use his razor on! Seeing mischief afoot, Apollo convinced the assembled congregants that what they needed was a good old-fashioned ritual bathing in the nearby stream. To get the full effect the bath must be had without garments—nude, naked, exposed. All the ladies complied except for the new convert who seemed ex-

tremely shy. Leucippus thought a little creative tucking might be his savior, but surrounded by a stream full of sun-kissed unencumbered female flesh, the knowledge of his maleness sprang instantly into view. Shortly thereafter, poor Leucippus was unmanned, unheaded, unarmed, and forever undone.

One by one Apollo disposed of the other suitors. At last the field was free for his wooing. It did not go well. Daphne wanted nothing to do with the god, no matter what particular persuasions he possessed. The nymph ran. The god gave chase. The nymph moved faster. Apollo increased his speed and slowly began to overtake the unwilling maiden. Daphne turned to her last resource. She prayed to Mother Earth to save her. As the fingertips of the god found the warm flesh of Daphne's retreating body, her prayers were answered. Her feet took root in the earth she stood on. Smooth bark spiraled upward to armor her flesh. Her hair pushed outward to become branches with leaves, all the while springing out to adorn the bare tendrils. Daphne had metamorphosed into a laurel tree. Apollo's hands fell away from the slim trunk. Small tears of defeat jeweled his eyelids. He sighed and left the nymph, who had gotten away from his lecherous desires, but not before he broke one thin branch, which he then formed into a circlet to ring his brow.. From then until now the laurel wreath has been used to paradoxically represent victory. So Daphne was rewarded with freedom rooted in the breast of the mother she worshipped and lusting Apollo got a hat.

PERSEPHONE. Hades was a lonely god. Down below the earth in the dim and dismal underworld that was his kingdom and his home he just could not meet women, at least of the still-breathing variety. So, he sat his throne alone and dreamed of having a queen, a female companion with whom to share the slow passing of the endless nights. Kore, who we know now as Persephone, was as young and pretty as the first small blooms of spring. She exuded such sweet joy and simple pleasure in the world around her that all those who found themselves in her company could not help but find themselves feeling the same joy and pleasure. It shouldn't be a surprise that this child of delight enjoyed the gifts of the natural world so much, for she was the daughter of Demeter, the goddess of the growing flora of the earth. One beautiful day with a sky as blue and unclouded as her sweet eyes, Persephone was with the Oceanids, those green-eyed daughters of Oceanus, playing in a meadow starred with wildflowers. As she bent to exult in the perfection of a narcissus bloom, the earth began to rumble and pitch. In an instant the ground split and the god of the underworld was belched through the breach in a chariot pulled by four black-as-coal stallions. Hades, the soil and sod shredding from his beard and shoulders, turned his dark gaze on Persephone and his hard hands took her soft shoulders to his chest. Back down through the cleft the chariot turned and the earth closed without hint of the kidnapping or the terrible disruption evident in even the slightest displaced petal or blade of grass.

The Oceanids, distracted for just the blink of a moment, wheeled to shout to their friend only to find the space that she had occupied empty. They called. They searched. Disheartened they reported to Demeter their sad and baffling news. Demeter was devastated. Her tender shoot-green spirit dulled to colorless and annihilated grey. And she searched in agony. Her feet shuffled from stone to yet unturned stone, and finding nothing, she continued in a grief the earth had never before witnessed. Exhausted, she returned to Olympus to share her woe and seek the aid of the other immortals. In the palace of the supreme, Demeter heard the fate of her daughter from Zeus's own lips. A bargain had been struck; Hades had been given permission to steal Persephone to use as his wife in order to keep him sitting on the drear throne of hell.

Demeter could not believe the horror of the words that slapped her ears. A bargain! An arranged abduction! In fury and abject despair she blasted the world with the ice that now enclosed her heart. The buds froze and failed, branches broke and fell, the grasses browned and choked in death. Winter swept the flowering earth and refused to release the warm breath of life. In the underworld, Persephone was listless and despondent for the world she had left behind. Hades in his clumsy way tried wooing to no avail. Cajoling met the same fate. Pleading only served to fill the halls of death with the whine of defeat. Persephone's body may be taken but her heart and soul would not yield. Heavens and earth were not the happy places of before.

The situation was grim and grew grimmer still. Zeus relented and struck another bargain but this time with the sorrowing mother. If Persephone had resided these months with Hades and in no way had shown the slightest consent to being there—not one drop of drink, not one morsel of sustenance, not one utterance of affirmation—then she could return to the earth's warm bosom. If she had, however, shown agreeableness in another form then she was doomed to stay. Demeter agreed, seeking any path to the release of her beloved daughter. Persephone had remained true in her refusal to accept anything from her captor, but in one infinitesimal way, once and only on that one occasion had she broken and taken anything from the lord of the afterlife's hand. After months of starvation she had retrieved a pomegranate from Hades's palm. It was ripe and full. It reminded her of the earth. It reminded her of her dear mother. She split the fruit and it spilled its seeds and three, small seeds had found their home on her tongue and down into her core. She had accepted by this tiny gesture of nostalgia for what had been.

Greatly vexed, Zeus could not let his earlier decision stand. A further bargain had to be made to spare the world the permanent freeze of winter and to keep his brother's backside firmly planted in the seat of the underworld. Persephone had eaten three seeds, so she must spend three months of every year in the confines of Hades. The other nine months she could return to the embrace of her mother. Grudgingly all parties accepted and from then on the earth has suffered a limited frost of three months in stark remembrance of Demeter's suffering loss and smiles in sunshine and rain the rest of the year. Persephone remained faithful to her husband and he, lord of death and forever endings, cheered and lived for that season of marital bliss when the rest of the universe shivered and prayed for the bright season to return. Remember, one man's, or god's, pomegranate is another man's poison.

PHAETON. Clymene was a nymph who had married Merops, the king of Egypt, but she had not always been such a faithful wife. She had had an affair with Helios the god of the sun. Clymene had gotten pregnant and conceived a son, Phaeton. Call it honesty or call it gloating, the nymph always and from the beginning told the son the truth of his parentage—"It might look like you're just the prince of the massive, powerful, and all mighty Egyptian empire, but no, you're better than that because you're the son of the sun!" It's hard for a boy to grow up in the royal palace knowing you should be hanging with the gods. Phaeton never lost an opportunity to tell his playmates about his divine heritage. Fights, arguments, and much teasing ensued. Clymene would attend to her son's battered knuckles and even more bruised ego by assuring him that it was true he was the son of Helios. More punching, more taunting, more disappointment, and even more motherly assurance followed. Finally, when Phaeton reached an age where he just couldn't take it anymore, he decided to settle it for once and all—he would find Helios himself and get the word straight from old sunshine's mouth.

Phaeton knew the direction he must travel—east to the sunrise. He traveled day after day, resting at night when dear old dad was off duty until at last he arrived at the very spot on the blank horizon where each morning the sun began its ascent into the heavens. And it was there that he discovered the gold-bright and almost blinding palace of his presumed father, Helios, just as that father was having Heliades hitch his gleaming saffron stallions to the flaming chariot of the sun. The boy was polite when he interrupted the sun god with his story. Helios for his part listened patiently, even as the morning awaited the sunrise. When Phaeton finished his tale, he nodded in recognition and maybe just a wee hint of happiness. Although not quite a "come to daddy" moment, Helios welcomed his son and, feeling just a bit guilty for all the lad had been through, promised by the river Styx to give him whatever he most desired—a promise once given that could not be rescinded. Impetuous teenager that he was, Phaeton knew instantly what he wanted—to drive the family car, the chariot of the sun, across the vault of heaven.

After all it was the family business, and he would have to learn it someday. Helios begged the boy to reconsider; there must be a million other things he might like instead. To live in the sun palace perhaps? An introduction to lots of "red-hot" nymphs? A visit to Mount Olympus? But no, Phaeton was sure about what he wanted and Helios was forced to give in. Phaeton would show everybody that laughed and called him a liar. He might just swoop down low enough to let them see him in his splendor and then they'd be sorry.

Helios, having certainly lost a little wattage, briefly instructed his son in proper sun chariot control and management. And without a doubt and just a little wave backward, Phaeton was off. The horses, through much practice, knew exactly what they were supposed to do and they liked doing it. Phaeton was so elated that he let the reins slip from his hands. The heretofore-docile steeds sensed that someone different and inexperienced was in the driver's seat. In an instant all the horsepower that had been directed at performing the well-known daily task was now set free to run willy-nilly across the sky. The chariot flew too high, brushing the very fabric of the heaven and burning holes that are still seen today as the Milky Way. The chariot stooped downward to the earth, setting forests alight and scorching deserts into existence. Rivers boiled. Flesh seared. The inhabitants of the planet cried out and Mother Earth, Gaea herself, felt their anguish and her own pains, too. She begged to stop the miscreant who rode in the vehicle that had been one of life-giving sunlight and now was burning with death-causing rays.

Zeus responded as quickly as he could draw a lightning bolt and sped it to its moving target. Phaeton was struck from the chariot and fell a cinder to the earth. At last, Helios was able to catch and bring under control his plunging ponies. Saddened, the next days were dimmer; the son regained was lost so soon. The earth healed but was scarred forever. Phaeton's half-sisters cried themselves to pine trees, their tears dropping and transforming into amber. His mother mourned her son's demise and her own rash honesty that had spurred him to this fate. Boys will be boys and fathers—mothers, too—must be carefull in what they pledge to give them. Gifts, no matter how bright and useful, can kill in childish hands.

MIDAS. Phrygia was a country ruled by a succession of kings named Midas (because Midas was the Phrygian term for "king"), but of all those rulers, only one is remembered today and he is so well remembered that even those who know the least will know his tale. King Midas was out hiking the rugged mountain trails of Phrygia one day when he found an old drunken fellow caught in the bramble thorns and unable to move. As a devotee of the god Dionysus, Midas was quickly able to identify the suffering captive. It was none other than Silenus, who in his inebriated wanderings had become separated from the god of wine's entourage and became entangled in his present predicament. Midas immediately set about to free the grateful reprobate. The good king then accompanied Silenus back to the relative safety of Dionysus's band and was greeted with loud halloos and happy thanks. As a gift for his service, Dionysus offered Midas a wish. The king pondered, but not for long, for swiftly he had concocted a scheme to solve all the troubles that assailed him. He wished that whatever he touched would be turned to gold. Without the faintest caution on the wisdom of such a gift, Dionysus granted it.

Midas, keeping his hands to himself, rushed home to test his new alchemical powers. On gaining the royal abode that in far Phrygia was considerably less than a palace, Midas stretched out his hand and placed his index finger on an apple. In a flash of stunning brilliance the fruit became an orb of solid gold. Joyously Midas touched, and grabbed and held chairs and tables, curtains, cushions, and even potted plants. Each and every item followed suit and changed its previous qualities into that rarest and most valuable of metals. Midas continued with his metallurgical Braille and soon almost the entire palace, for now it truly was so much more than a humble residence, from columns to lintels, from floor to roof, was a construction of the precious substance. The only non-gold features of the entire house were the occupants, and Midas came so close to hugging or kissing them, but he showed at least this small restraint. Maybe living flesh would not succumb to his heavy melt massage, he wondered. Perhaps only inanimate objects were subject to his gift?

Midas decided to put it to the test before having a loving embrace with his wife or children or even shaking hands with one of the servants. He rushed to the barnyard and took a chicken into his trembling arms. White feathers and pink flesh were now the weight, color, and substance of gold. He would never be able to touch another living person, another living thing! And suddenly he realized that as that first apple had changed, so would all his food. He could spend it, luxuriate in it, but he could not eat it! The blessing, which had transformed base elements into that material men dreamed of, had quickly transformed itself into a curse.

Headlong Midas rushed through field and forest, back to Dionysus. He begged the god to take his gift away. Dionysus relented but warned the king that all he had touched to this point would once again assume its former quality. What good is gold if it can't be eaten, if every embrace was the touch of death? Dionysus relented and a chastened Midas returned to his home to enjoy the simple pleasures and pains of his life.

But this isn't all that's written about King Midas. The King truly loved the rustic life and all the divinities that were most comfortable there. Just as he had made the acquaintance of the god Dionysus, he had also befriended the god of wild Arcadia, Pan. Midas especially loved the music Pan played, being too old and happily married to participate in his pursuit of female flesh. He could lie for hours in a forest glade or even a sheep pasture and listen to the enchantment of the syrinx. He had given up his golden touch, but basking in the music of the panpipes he felt the same richness he had felt before. Pan was equally pleased with his musical acumen and boasted of his abilities to Midas and the nymphs that often circled him enraptured. One nymph carried the boast all the way to the ears of Apollo. Specifically, Pan had proclaimed that he was an even better musician that great Apollo himself. Apollo was not pleased and sought out the goat-footed god among the Phrygian crags. He found him relaxing with his instrument in hand and challenged Pan to a musical contest. Pan agreed to the competition; he was ready to have his chops measured against the master of the lyre. The gods faced off and all the hastily assembled nymphs, dryads, shepherds, and mountain men were assigned the role of judges. Midas sat there too among the excited concertgoers ready to lend his ear and voice to the proceedings.

Pan began and never had the old goat-faced god played better. His trills and runs and the sublime colors of his tune entered the throng and truly transported them. Apollo smugly listened and nonchalantly took his stance before the crowd. His fingers rushed across the strings, an arpeggio divine! He delicately plucked as drops of nectar filled the ears of all the assembled. Apollo's music was gorgeous. Pan's had been lovely but of all the judges only one thought his the better of Apollo's. That one loyal but mistaken listener was none other than Midas. Apollo graciously thanked his audience and blessed them with small favors and then turned his attention to Midas. With a flick of his finger on the string of his instrument Apollo changed the shape of Midas's ears. In place of his human organs he now had the ears of an ass! Midas ran away, yet again, from the attention of a divinity. This time there was no appeal to any of the powers to turn back the punishment. All Midas could do was pull a Phrygian cap over his deformed head and keep it there.

But no man can keep a hat on his head forever. His hair grew shaggy, itching, and uncomfortable; he just had to go to his barber. The royal barber had not laid shears on Midas's head in many a day and was pleased to see the frantic king. As King Midas placed his bottom on the stool, the barber reached to remove Midas's cap and immediately had his hand slapped back. First the barber must swear on pain of death to never reveal what he was about to witness. Assuredly, he would never do anything to bring dishonor on his king and, with that assurance, Midas revealed his secret. The barber, in a state of shock, performed his surgery on the king's locks in record time and Midas paid and left with his haircut hidden beneath his cap. The barber could hardly believe what his eyes had shown him, and he ached to share the secret. But no, he would hold his tongue.

Days passed and the burden the barber bore did not lessen. It instead grew greater, as if he carried not the ears of an ass on his head but the entire ass on his back. It was too much for the poor man to bear. He just had to say it out loud, but he would be cautious and say it outside any hearing. He wandered far with shovel in hand and at last selected a lonely, empty spot where no one could ever hear what he was about to say. As a further precaution the barber dug a hole, getting down on his knees placed his head in the hole and whispered—"Midas has the ears of an ass!" Satisfied, he covered the hole and trekked home and out of the story. But the ears of the earth heard and spoke the shameful secret to the ants and the ants to the beetles and the beetles to the grasshoppers and on and on until the reeds standing at the riverbank heard and as the wind blew across their open mouths they spread it the world—*Midas has the ears of an ass!* Poor Midas learned even the most private of follies has a life in public. And once out in the common air, no cap can hide it.

ATALANTA. When King Iasus of Arcadia was informed that his wife had just given birth to a beautiful, bouncing baby girl, he was furious. Sons! He wanted sons! In is anger he ordered his servants to take the newborn to the slopes of Mount Parthenion and let nature take its course—which nature did in an unexpected way. A big she-bear happened along and found the crying baby. Far from making a quick meal of the tender little girl, the mama bear gently lifted the bundle in her jaws and carried her home to place with her very own cubs. The baby, named Atalanta before being disposed of on the hillside, prospered at the teat of the bear and learned resilience and skills with her furry littermates. One day while out romping with her bear siblings, she was chanced upon by a band of hunters who adopted her after first shooing the cubs away. The hunters raised her in the ways of the wild woods, expanding the teaching she had already received from the bears, and she grew to young womanhood as a prodigious hunter, almost the rival of Artemis herself. She also grew up chaste and with plans to remain that way with yet another nod to the virgin huntress.

MAMA?

In Calydon, a neighboring kingdom, a great hunt had been declared by the young Prince Meleager. The Calydonian forests had been plagued by a huge and ferocious boar, and Meleager decided to rid the world of the tusker while having a good time of it. He summoned all the heroes of Greece to join in the sport and many of them answered in assent. Jason, the commander of the *Argo* and winner of the Golden Fleece; Castor and Polydeuces, who had been Jason's shipmates; Peleus, the father of Achilles; and

Nestor, who would later be the oldest warrior at Troy, were just some of the hunters who would try their hands and spears against the great boar. Among all the bronze-hard, scarred, and battle-tested men arrived a young woman to take her place among them—Atalanta. Immediately the grumbling began and the men took their protests to Meleager, but Meleager was instantly smitten by the huntress and declared that Atalanta was welcome to join the hunt.

Into the forest the bold hunters carefully picked their way, some alone, some in groups of one or two, to track and bring down the dread pig. Meleager stayed close to Atalanta and the skills she had learned from earliest infancy proved invaluable in reading the silent language of spoor and scat. It wasn't long until Atalanta had sussed out the lair of the boar. One by one the hunters gathered to root their prey out of its hiding place, but sensing danger, the gigantic beast charged out to meet his adversaries. Atalanta was the first to thrust her spear into his hairy side, and only the armor of his ribs kept the point from finding the beating heart. Others poked and prodded, but Meleager stood his ground and found the boar's throat with his spear, ending the reign of terror he had inflicted on the denizens of the woods.

In an act of generosity inspired by infatuation Meleager presented Atalanta with the hide and tusks of the defeated monster. King Iasus was told the tales of his abandoned daughter's decidedly unladylike prowess, and he had her brought back to the bosom of the family. She was not so bad for a girl. But for the father who wanted so much for a son, he wasted no time in treating Atalanta just like a daughter and a princess to boot. Iasus demanded that she must marry and get to the nuptials pretty quick. Atalanta was shocked but agreed with one condition: She would only marry a man who could beat her in a footrace and anyone who challenged and lost would lose more than a prize princess; they would forfeit their life. Iasus consented—he would gain one impressive son-in-law and it would keep his executioner occupied.

As beautiful and skillful as Princess Atalanta was, nobody seemed interested in taking the challenge—except for a young prince named Melanion. The prince, although a strong runner, wasn't content to just rely on his legs. He decided to enlist the aid of some real powers. Melanion prayed to Aphrodite to help him win the object of his love. The goddess was moved by the young man's entreaties and provided him with a gift—three golden apples. With this unfair advantage, Melanion went to King Iasus and formally accepted Atalanta's challenge. The day of the contest arrived. The athletes glistened in the sun, their oiled bodies twitching to be off. Go! And they were off! Straining every muscle, Melanion took the early lead and struggled mightily to keep it. Atalanta, with smooth easy strides, was over-taking him, and he knew it was time release his first secret weapon. He dropped a golden apple in the path. Atalanta screeched to a stop to examine and take the precious fruit. Melanion increased his lead and the princess, with apple in hand, set off behind him. When once again the prince could hear her footsteps getting nearer, he deployed his second apple, and Atalanta stopped dead in her tracks to retrieve it.

Melanion used every ounce of strength to push ahead but even with his unfair advantage, Atalanta was still catching up. At last, with the finish line in sight and the weighted down Atalanta breathing hard on his neck, Melanion tossed his third and final apple. Atalanta stopped again to gather up the glittering prize as Melanion crossed the finish line. Atalanta, huntress, princess, and golden fruit picker, was wed to Melanion the crafty prince. Whether or not they lived happily ever after is not recorded, but we can be sure it was a marriage that never left a challenge unmet.

DAEDALUS AND ICARUS.

There were gods in ancient Greece who were blessed with abilities that took them far beyond the realm of normal human experience and there was one man whose genius and skill sometimes made him the equal of those gods—and sometimes just as tragic. The man was Daedalus and he was a builder, but what a builder, fabricator, engineer, inventor, designer, and creator he was. Problems set before him were spurs to his abilities. He solved those problems and sometimes in the offing created new and bigger ones. Daedalus was also a jealous master of his craft. He fled his native Athens after throwing his nephew Talos, who was also his apprentice, from the top of the Acropolis. Talos had committed the grave sin of inventing the saw and his proud uncle just could not allow another inventor in the family, especially one who showed such extraordinary promise that he might one day equal or rival his master. Daedalus and his son Icarus went to Crete to seek the patronage of King Minos.

Minos was a powerful and wealthy ruler who seemed to have no end of projects for Daedalus to work on, but it was the queen, the alluring Pasiphae, that offered the builder his greatest challenge. Poor Pasiphae had fallen in love, or rather, lust with a bull. The bull was no ordinary bovine; he was a gift from Poseidon and had arrived dripping from the sea. His broad head with its horns curving in imitation of the crescent moon was the most handsome head that ever graced a bull's body. The bull's muscles bulged under his sleek black coat like the very equal of the god that sent him. And his manhood was a display that even the most chaste of women gaped at in admiration. The Minoans held bulls sacred and Pasiphae fell to his charms. To Daedalus the queen took her deep desires, and Daedalus was up for the challenge.

He fashioned the model of a cow whose beauty made women blush and strong men weep at the wonder of it. Pasiphae was strategically placed inside the hollow body of the horned simulacrum and, when introduced to the magnificent bull, the queen was pacified. Nine months after the consummation, Queen Pasiphae gave birth to a monster—the body of a normal albeit powerful human crowned with the head of the bull that fathered him. The shame of it, and the need to hide it, drew Pasiphae to Daedalus again. This time he must build an enclosure to confine this creature, dubbed the Minotaur from then on. The builder knew that such a prison could not just rely on strong walls; eventually such a creature would grow strong enough to breach even the strongest stone. It would need to be a dungeon that used craft to hold the beast. He fashioned the labyrinth to do the work of concealment and confinement. It would be a series of stone-lined underground chambers and hallways that even the most intelligent of men would find themselves lost in, let alone a poor dumb beast. What happened to the Minotaur locked away in his puzzle? That is another story, one for a young Athenian named Theseus to solve, but Daedalus, for all his wits and abilities, became a prisoner of the furious cuckold King Minos. He was locked away in a high chamber, a tower impossible to climb down from or to escape through the one locked and heavily guarded door. His only companion was his son Icarus.

Icarus was a good and devoted son. The child was always ready to aid his sire in every project, but was never to take the reigns of those endeavors. Icarus would never ever be his father's equal or have close to a fraction of his skill. He was a boy of moderate, if not less than moderate, intellectual ability. But no matter his limitations, he was a good and loving companion and truly the one thing in all the world Daedalus loved. Trapped in King Minos's stone eyrie, the genius was not defeated, because with even the most meager of materials he was still possessed of the greatest tool, his own mind. They had been provided candles, because Minos still wanted Daedalus's services and he would need to see, and little else except for those materials needed to accomplish very specific and limited tasks. For years the tower had been occupied by birds and their feathers were still in abundance. With what little they had Daedalus would build their route to escape. Taking the wax and the feathers, Daedalus constructed two pairs of wings that only birds or possibly gods possessed, a pair for each of the captives.

He instructed his son in the science of flight, because even though he had not done it (nor any other man before him), he still had spent hours in observation of birds and understood the lessons of aerodynamics. If Icarus would follow his direction, their escape would be as smooth as an eagle's glide. There was only one paramount hazard to beware of: Do not fly too close to the sun, for the heat of Helios's chariot would melt the wax and destroy the fragile wings. With that the aeronauts jumped through the casement and were away from the grip of the vengeful king. The wings worked like miracles and in moments the duo were flying as ably as any creature born with the appendages. They flapped and soared. They swooped and floated. They could not help but feel the joy of rushing through the free air with clouds their only impediment. It would be no time before they would make landfall on the Greek mainland and achieve safety from King Minos. Filled with the thrill of freedom, Icarus did the one thing he had been warned against— an act of hubris committed with the greatest happiness a man could ever know. Icarus flew higher and higher still to approach the glory of the sun. The wax grew soft and softer; feathers molted and drifted to the sea so far below. Daedalus shouted his warnings, but the boy was breathing in the ether of heaven. At last, the wings failed and fell away, and Icarus, still caught in rapture, fell to his death so far below in Poseidon's waves. In abject grief, Daedalus made it to the shore and found new employ and even ultimate revenge on King Minos (indoor plumbing achieved the boiling of royalty like a crab in a pot), but he never recovered from the loss of his son. Each day he awakened in the morning blaze and each day he cursed what everyone else rejoiced, the ascent of Helios's chariot—the sun that had taken his.

2. THE HEROES

Every culture seems to love a good yarn about men, and the occasional woman, doing seemingly impossible deeds for glorious outcomes. Our ancient Greeks not only told those tales but made them such good ones that thousands of years later we are still enjoying them. Of course, our ancient heroes had a decided advantage over many of the fellows that came after them because most of our ancients were *demigods*—the product of one human and one divine parent. This condition of "semi-divinity" not only gave them abilities no ordinary man might ever achieve but also gave them direct access to a god and that parent-god's sometimes considerable aid. Of course, sometimes our heroes had to fight off the curses of other gods offended by the "accident" of their birth, but it takes a little vinegar in the brew to make the sweetness come out. Their advantages, disadvantages, luck, and pluck all make for some great stories!

PERSEUS. Acrisius the king of Argos was a religious man who heeded the oracles. One such prophetess had declared that he would meet his end by the hand of a son of his house. Acrisius had an only daughter named Danae and it seemed to him only politic to shut that daughter in an impregnable room of bronze so she would remain without a consort, and therefore she became an impregnable daughter. No room was unreachable by Zeus when he had caught sight of a woman he fancied, and he fancied Danae. Zeus transformed himself into a shower and penetrated the tiny cracks and fissures of the dungeon. Danae bathed exultantly in this divine spray and nine months later gave birth to Perseus. The king was mortified, terrified, and fit to be tied, but it was poor innocent Danae and her newborn that were truly tried and convicted.

Acrisius put them in a large chest—comfortably furnished with pillows, blankets, and nourishing tidbits—and had it padlocked and tossed into the waves to let the sea act as executioner. But the wind and waves were merciful and the ill-suited watercraft washed up on the sands of the island of Seriphos where it was found by Dictys the fisherman. Dictys liberated the captive mother and child and took them to the court of King Polydectes who was happy to receive these mysterious sailors. Perseus was cast adrift by one king and raised by another. Of course, kings being kings this fellow also had certain intentions. Polydectes had a yen for the fair Danae and the fair Danae did not return the currency of love or desire. She thwarted his every move until Polydectes decided he would just

court someone else, but courting is a costly proposition and some-
body has got to pay. Enter the penniless Perseus. The head of
Medusa would certainly make a lovely wedding gift, declared Polydectes, and Perseus had no recourse but to agree.

Perseus was a young and likely hero, but where to begin? Lucky for
him he had a powerful ally among the divines. Athena was ready to
throw in her lot with any young buck who was willing to take on her
enemy Medusa—remember, Medusa had defiled Athena's temple
by having a little tête-à-tête with Poseidon in its confines and a wise
goddess never forgets. Athena warned the lad never to look into
Medusa's eyes for they possessed the power to turn men into stone,
but not to fear for she had a gift for him. She gave him a polished
shield and all he had to do was to gaze into its mirror-like surface to
spy his adversary. Hermes also chimed in with some appropriate
gifts—a sharp sickle to liberate the Gorgon's head from her neck, a
leather bag to bring it home in, directions to the lair of the Graiae
sisters (who knew Medusa's whereabouts) and to a pair of winged
sandals (so he could fly about like Hermes Junior), and the lend of
a *tarnhelm* from Hades (which renders the wearer invisible).

Off to Mount Atlas to the cave of the Graiae sisters Perseus went. The sisters suffered from an almost fatal lack of beauty—they were *ugly*, and what rendered them even less attractive was the single eye they had between them that they passed from one to another. Perseus had every intention of being civil, but the obnoxious siblings would have none of it, and our hero was forced to take desperate measures—he snatched the eye from the nearest sister and held it ransom until they delivered the information he needed. He was off in no time to the Stygian swamps to gather his further accoutrements from the nymphs. Then he sped his winged feet to the island sanctuary of Medusa.

Perseus was as ready a hero, as ever there was one—loaded with weaponry and advice—when he arrived to do in the Gorgon. He stalked the monster's lair and found her cave. He donned the tarn-helm and positioned the shield where he could see without looking at her directly. Perseus pursued his advantage and swooshed his sickle and the grim fruit, covered with writhing serpents, came flying off. Out of the newly opened passageway of the neck came the winged Pegasus and his brother, Chrysaor, who would grow up to be a mighty warrior. Thus Medusa gave life to the children of Poseidon with her death.

Perseus spared nary a moment to plop the grisly trophy into the leather bag and to take steps in the air to home. Along the way he couldn't help but notice a comely lass chained to a rock by the sea with nothing to protect her but her own naked skin. On soaring in for a closer look, a purely academic gaze, he saw the terrible sea monster bearing down to make of her a quick dinner. Out with the head of Medusa and the leviathan became instant statuary. Freed from being the entrée, the lady was released from her bonds and explained that she was the Princess Andromeda, nearly sacrificed because of her mama's vanity. Her mother, Cassiopeia, had boasted that she was prettier than the sea nymphs and these girls had complained to Poseidon. Poseidon released the monster on Joppa, the seat of King Cepheus and Cassiopeia's kingdom, to do some damage and was only willing to call it off if the royals were willing to offer the princess for supper.

Amid the general joy and hubbub, Perseus asked for Andromeda's hand in marriage. The king and queen were more than happy to consent but Phineus, another young suitor was not, and he went home for his army. Perseus once again put Medusa's noggin on display and, where there had been ranks of troops ready to attack, now there was a sculpture garden. The marriage was celebrated and the newlyweds headed for Sephoria.

But things were awry on the island kingdom of Polydectes, as well. The king's fancy for Danae had grown to the point where he was now a danger to Perseus's mother. She had fled with the trusty Dictys and they were now besieged by Polydectes and his men-at-arms in a small and vulnerable temple. Just in the nick of time, Perseus arrived with his all-powerful weapon to save the day. Out comes Medusa's head to do to Polydectes and his honchos what had been done to Phineus and his before. After all, Polydectes had asked for the head as a present, and as the wind and rain would slowly erode his stony form for many years to come, he could rest assured that he had received the value of it.

With great gratitude Perseus placed Dictys the loyal and valiant fisherman on the throne of Sephoria—never a bad idea to have one who intimately knows the sea in charge of an island kingdom—and gathered the rest of the family for a triumphant return to Argos. King Acrisius now quite stooped and twisted with age was still afraid of his male offspring and fled to avoid meeting his famous grandson. Unfortunately, he fled to the city of Larissa where Perseus had already been invited to participate in the late ruler's funeral games. The Fates are never to be put off their weaving. He became the unwitting catcher of a discus tossed by the boy he sought to escape.

Argos was without a king and the people hoped to conscript Perseus to sit the throne, but the hero, in probably his most heroic act, refused. He had had enough of kings and courts and took his family to the east. His son Perses would later found the Persian Empire, but Perseus wanted nothing but a simple life. He returned the sandals and tarnhelm to the Stygian nymphs and presented the head of Medusa to his benefactress, Athena. She fixed it to her breastplate— the all-protecting *aegis*. Perseus and Andromeda happily retired from mythological pursuits and eventually became the greatest heroes of every true tale—ordinary people.

BELLEROPHON. Some people, no matter how smart or good looking or connected, just seem to collect troubles like a ship collects barnacles—scrape one and another seems to take its spot. Such a man was Bellerophon. He fled his native Corinth after killing another man. Was it murder or an accident? No one was quite sure other than after a dispute one man died and one man left for parts unknown. So, Bellerophon arrived in the city of Tiryns ready to start a new and pacific life, but his plans almost immediately went awry when as a guest of the palace he was spotted by Queen Stheneboea, the wife of King Proteus. As she eagle-eyed the young man, she had adultery seeping through the whorls and canyons of her brain. Bellerophon recoiled when he was pounced upon; he didn't come to Tiryns for trouble. But sometimes this kind of trouble finds you no matter where you hide.

Stheneboea did not take this young bravo's rejection with good grace. She decided that if the lad did not want her, he probably did not want to live much longer. The queen informed the king that the beautiful young guest had attempted to rape her and she just managed to escape his lecherous violence. Proteus was outraged, but what could he do? Bellerophon was a guest of his house and there were the strictest proscriptions against harming a guest. If Proteus laid a glove on the boy he could bring down a curse on his entire house. But he could send Bellerophon on to his father-in-law King Iobates of Lycia with a note detailing the fellow's crimes, and

Iobates could extract justice from the miscreant's bones. Bellerophon would be the messenger of his own execution—signed, sealed, and delivered for his crimes. On reaching Lycia, Bellerophon delivered his own death sentence to King Iobates, but Iobates now had his dilemma to resolve for the criminal was now his guest. The king hit on a clever idea: He would give Bellerophon some incredibly dangerous, suicidal task to do and that would finish the business. Nobody would be violating any rules of hosting.

Enter the Chimera, a fire-breathing monster with the head of a lion, the body of a goat, and the tail of a snake. This beauty was holed up in a cave and only came out to lay waste the countryside and make lunch of the king's subjects. Bellerophon was politely bid to dispatch the evil beast posthaste, and as a guest he could not refuse a little payback for such hospitality. Like any young hero, Bellerophon set off with his deadly "vorpal" blade in hand and not the faintest idea what to do with his head. But Bellerophon truly was innocent, and so Athena took pity on him. She told him that the winged horse Pegasus favored a particular spring for refreshment and, while enjoying a cool drink, he would be vulnerable. Bellerophon could sneak up on him and place a golden bridal

over his nose, and the horse will be his to command. Bellerophon followed the goddess's instruction and was flying the friendly skies in no time. But those skies turned decidedly unfriendly when polluted with the smog above the Chimera's lair. Bellerophon had to decide how to attack the beast, utilizing Pegasus to his best advantage. A full frontal assault, swooping in under the clouds with his sword swinging, sounded like a plan until one considered the blow-torch breath of the Chimera. Maybe just flying in from behind and dismounting to attack was the most effective strategy, but that wasn't really using the winged horse to the best advantage. No, an attack from the air, planted firmly on the back of his aerial advantage, was the way to do it and Bellerophon cottoned on just what to do.

He gathered lumps of lead, and weighted with these crude weapons, he mounted Pegasus and was off to the battle. And a short battle it turned out to be for the horse and rider stayed well above the flames of the Chimera's noxious breath. But when that mouth was gaping with a blast, Bellerophon dropped the lead into the open maw. The metal melted, running down into the Chimera's gullet and soon the creature, filled to the brim with molten lead, expired. Bellerophon returned to Lycia the conquering hero—and the continuing problem. Iobates was elated and deflated in the same moment. At last, the king concluded that he must continue with the punishment his son-in-law wanted exacted from Bellerophon, so he placed upon the young man's shoulders what seemed like another insolvable task—the savage Solymians and their even more frightening allies, the Amazons, were massing to attack the kingdom, and Bellerophon was commanded to thwart their conquering aims.

Back in the saddle again, Bellerophon concocted an even bolder aerial assault on this mass of approaching enemies. He gathered sharp stones and heavy projectiles and proceeded to bomb the Solymians and Amazons while safe above and out of reach of bow-shot. The hellish rain of rocks soon demoralized the attackers, who wondered, if the Lycians could do this much damage with one man, what could they do if they had an entire cavalry to take to the skies? Across the border the wannabe conquerors retreated. Once again, atop his blazing white-winged steed, Bellerophon went riding back to the palace of King Iobates. Enough was enough; Iobates figured the kid had more than proved himself. The death sentence was torn up, and instead Bellerophon was sentenced, marry Princess Philonoe. Bellerophon was now the heir to the kingdom, which seemed only fair after all he had done to keep it safe. So was it at last happily ever after?

After all these adventures with supernatural creatures, battles with frightening foes, reversals of fortune, and simply surviving to glorious success, Bellerophon figured that maybe he could get a bit more mileage out of Pegasus before he put him out to pasture. He would sit the flying thoroughbred for one last great undertaking—they would fly to Mount Olympus and say a howdy-do to the gods. Up and up they flew, passing clouds and even the boldest hawks. Higher and higher into the rarefied air that held the gods in the sweetest breath of heaven, the winged pair ascended. At the very gates of Olympus, Zeus spotted the foolhardy interloper and, in an expression of understatement, issued forth not a thunderbolt, after all he had no wish to harm the unoffending horse, but a gadfly. The gadfly with one small swift bite sent Bellerophon's plans crashing down and the hero with it. Pegasus flew off, free of the rein again and Bellerophon returned swiftly to the mundane earth. Broken and chastened, Bellerophon lived a long life as a hermit, not a hero, not a king. He had enough of the machinations of men and the retaliations of gods. He was satisfied to let only his dreams have wings and then only for short flights close to the ground.

THESEUS. Aegeus, the king of Athens, was sonless and

I JUST SAY IT — I DON'T UNDERSTAND WHAT I SAY.

brokenhearted at the prospect of not having an heir. He traveled to the oracle at Delphi for some prophetic advice. But oracles being oracles, Aegeus couldn't quite understand exactly what she said. On the journey back to Athens, he stopped at Troezen where he told King Pittheus his trouble and rehearsed the garbled message from the seer at Delphi. Pittheus understood the message—somewhere on this journey Aegeus would conceive a son and that son was going to be one big hero—but he kept his understanding to himself. That night he put on a feast augmented with lots of fine wine, and when Aegeus was suitably liquored, he put the Athenian to bed with his daughter Aethra. When the morning arrived Aegeus discovered that he had not only a roaring hangover but a pretty bedmate as well. Aegeus may have had difficulty deciphering oracular mutterings, but he could certainly put two and two together in the bedroom. He took Aethra along with him a short way on his path to home and stopped at a suitably sized but inconspicuous stone beside the road. Under the stone he placed the sandals off his own feet and the sword of Cecrops, the first king of Athens. Aegeus instructed Aethra that if she delivered a son from their inebriated liaison to bring him to this spot to lift the stone and let him retrieve the cache before sending him to Athens and dear old dad.

Theseus was the outcome of this prophesied carnal meeting, but Theseus also had another father, a divine one. By some strange alchemy of myth he was also carrying the genetic material of Poseidon. He was not only the heir to the throne of Athens but also a chip off the old god of the sea. This was a pretty decent start for our young hero, and he grew by leaps and bounds into a robust teenager, bursting with potential. Aethra took him to the appointed rock. Theseus lifted and found, instead of a stray lizard or hiding snake, the booty that would secure his place in the dynasty to Athens. So it was bye-bye, Mama, and off to the big city.

The road to Athens was not an easy one and Theseus encountered obstacle after belligerent obstacle. First he had to deal with Periphetes, a son of Hephaestus, who was lame like his father, but his condition did not keep him from robbing and dispatching all who came down the road with his big brass club. Theseus dealt with Periphetes with his own weapon. Then the boy met Sinis, another vicious criminal who liked to tie his victims between a couple of bent pine trees and let them fly, splitting the poor captive into several pieces. Theseus let him experience the pine ride. Then he came across Sciron, who forced people to bend down and wash his nasty feet, and when they were in a suitable crouch, he punted them over the cliff into the waiting maw of a people-eating turtle. Soon after making Theseus's acquaintance Sciron became the turtle chow. At Crommyon, Theseus made bacon out of a ferocious sow that had left the hog lot to terrorize the countryside. Kerkyon, the king of Eleusis, was fond of challenging likely lads along the road to a cage match and then wrestling them to death. Two men went in but only Theseus came out. And if this litany of murderers and miscreants wasn't enough, Procrustes and his bed just might put them all to rest. Procrustes took wayfarers to his hovel and put them in his ill-sized bed. If they were too short he stretched them; if they were too long he chopped them to size. Needless to say, all guests were put permanently to sleep. Theseus took Procrustes to the bed he made and made him lie in it. All tucked in, Procrustes closed his eyes forever.

At last, Theseus reached the capitol of

Greek civilization and, far from tired from his travels, he was ready for more. Aegeus the king had not let time fly without trying to make another successor to his throne. Medea, the witch and angry ex-wife of Jason, had married the Aegeus and lo-and-behold presented him with a baby, Medus. When Theseus arrived swinging his daddy's sword and slapping dirt in his papa's shoes, she was none too pleased, especially since Theseus had a couple of years on Medus and was next in line for the royal seat. She caught Aegeus's ear before he had time to truly register the lad and sent him out to take care of the Cretan bull that had been captured by Heracles and escaped the farm to trample the good folk of Marathon. In no time the steaks were being served up to the happy people. Next she thought a more direct approach might be better, so she poisoned Theseus's wine during a feast. But this time her machinations resulted in Aegeus's recognition of his true heir, for there, on the young hero's hip, was the one and only sword of Cecrops. Theseus was what he purported to be—the son of Aegeus.

Though Medea did not succeed, fate and hubris might. For years Athens had been forced to pay tribute to King Minos of Crete. Minos's son had been murdered in Athens and it seemed to have been a state-sanctioned execution. The tribute exacted was a terrible one—each year seven young men and seven young women were selected to sail to Crete and were forced into the labyrinth, the prison of the Minotaur (the illegitimate and ill-formed lovechild of Queen Pasiphae) constructed by Daedalus, and to become the monster's eventual meal. Theseus, ever the hero, volunteered to be one of the youths. He wouldn't take for an answer, even when Aegeus pleaded with him to reconsider. The king was forced to give in but with one proviso: The ship always sailed with black sails in mourning for this lost bouquet of Athenian youth, but if Theseus succeeded in his quest, then the ship must return with the billowing white sails of victory. Theseus agreed and the ship and its cargo sailed off to the dread island.

Upon reaching the island of Crete, Minos met the ill-fated youngsters and surveyed their worth. The king addressed them in an arrogant and abusive fashion, to which Theseus could not fail to reply. He let old Minos know that he may not get the outcome with this sacrifice that he desired; instead, with the aid of his own protector and father, Poseidon, that old Minotaur just might be eating his next meal in hell. Rebuked by the whelp, Minos set Theseus a test. The king pulled a gold ring from one of the collections displayed on his royal fingers and tossed it into the deep. Maybe Theseus and his protector could find that. Without hesitation, Theseus dove into waves and in no time Poseidon had the Nereids assisting in the search and retrieval. Theseus came splashing upward with the gold ring twirling on his finger.

Minos was not amused by this jewelry rescue but his daughter Ariadne was more than a little excited by the handsome Athenian. In fact, she decided that Theseus was one meal that her horned and hairy half-brother was not going to have. She sought Theseus out before he entered the labyrinth; it was a deadly puzzle, even if one avoided the Minotaur. Once within its halls and passages, one would be lost forever. Ariadne presented Theseus with a ball of red thread—curious maybe, ingenious certainly. If one unspooled the thread slowly as one went along then one could retrace the route backward into the light of day. Theseus thanked the young princess for this gift of love, a gift that directly countermanded the will of her father, and entered the labyrinth. It was not long before Theseus heard the snorts and hoof clacking of the Minotaur, whose flared nostrils caught the scent of dinner long before the Athenian could have sniffed out the even more pungent odor of the man-bull. There in the dim dusty half-light of the labyrinth, hero and monster met in mortal combat. The sword of Cecrops that Theseus had secreted under his chiton found butchery to be done and the pathetic beast, shunned by everyone and feared by all, found death in the prison that was his home.

Following the thread back from where he came, Theseus exited the maze with the bloodied bull's horns as his trophy. Quickly he packed Ariadne and the liberated Athenians back on the ship and hurriedly set sail for Athens. Inexplicably, the homeward-bound barque dropped anchor off the island of Naxos. Provisions and water they had plenty and they made haste to ease the fears of their loved ones. Why the unscheduled stop? Motive is everything and in this case motive is unknowable. In an act of the most callous ingratitude, Theseus marooned Ariadne on the isle, though she had betrayed her own family to help save him. Theseus sailed on, but Ariadne eventually made an even better match than the prince of Athens—she was discovered by that ever wandering god, Dionysus, and it was he who returned love to the abandoned princess and marriage was his gift to her.

Everyday, Aegeus took to the cliffs outside Athens to scan the horizon for the returning ship of doom. Every day he returned home without having had sight of it. Of course, if the ship returned with black sails unfurled, it was news he would rather not receive and terribly it was the news Aegeus did receive as he sat his perch on the crags above the sea. Theseus, in his haste and extreme thoughtlessness, had forgotten to change the sails from the saturated shade of death to victory white. Old Aegeus was struck with grief that he had never known before—to gain a son like this and to lose him so quickly. In an act of despair he threw himself from the cliffs to the sea crashing below. From then until this very day that sea, the Aegean, bears his name as so long ago it bore his broken body.

The triumph of Theseus's return was muted somewhat by the untimely and unexpected death of his father, but in the days to come he was crowned king of Athens and sought to be a good king. He welcomed skilled people to become citizens of the city. He instituted games for the amusement of the populace. Athens prospered and Theseus grew bored. He went off on adventures that were not always the most beneficial: he defeated the Amazons and wed their queen Hippolyta. He buddied up with his fellow king Pirithous and abducted Helen, who was subsequently rescued by the her brothers Castor and Pollux, the so-called Dioscuri. He and Pirithous hadn't learned their lesson after the business with Helen and went down into Hades to abduct Persephone—Pirithous did not return and Theseus only made it back by the saving grace of his friend Heracles. He got involved in the Theban troubles and offered poor blind Oedipus a place to rest his dying head. He even married the deserted Ariadne's sister Phaedra after his wife Hippolyta died, and it was this marriage that eventually led to his downfall.

Theseus and Hippolyta had a son Hippolytus and the boy was deeply devoted to the goddess Artemis. Aphrodite, who happened to be deeply devoted to Hippolytus, was not pleased and turned Eros loose with his arrows. One well-aimed dart and Phaedra was now in love with Hippolytus. Hippolytus had only one love and that was for the chaste goddess of the hunt and the life of the forest chase. He spurned his stepmother Phaedra. Crazy with love, the queen hanged herself. Theseus, who understood about half of what had transpired and not the helpful half, cursed his son, who fled, only to have the curse realized by a slapping tidal wave from Theseus's other father, Poseidon.

Theseus was a broken man. He could hardly sink any deeper in his grief when he lost the throne of Athens to Menesthius, a well-placed noble who had returned to the city with the Dioscuri. Theseus sailed toward Crete, where he had made his name so long ago to the court of his brother-in-law, Minos, his enemy long dead. He never arrived, because he was blown instead to the island of Scyros, where the king

welcomed but feared even this depressed and ancient man, for few could ever reach the heights of his heroism. From its heights the king pushed the unaware Theseus, and so the mighty slayer of monsters fell. In historic times, Theseus's bones were eventually returned to the city of his triumphs and tragedies, but bones or no, the age of heroes had long passed.

JASON. As a babe in arms, Jason was already a victim of ancient Greek mythological family values. His father, King Eason, and mother, Alcimede of Iolcos, had been murdered in a coup carried out by the king's brother Pelias. Pelias had thought his job of usurpation had been completed and all the family members had been butchered, but baby J had been snuck out of the realm to eventually be in the care of and mentored by Chiron, the urbane and professorial centaur. The new king only found out about his existence from an oracle that warned him about the eventual arrival of a one-sandaled man. From then on Pelias was fetishistic about men's footwear. After a childhood spent in exile, Jason came home to Iolcos, having first lost a sandal in the Anaurus River. All Pelias's fears had come home with the returning of the young man, and he had to come up with a plan to thwart the Fates. The Golden Fleece was the answer. The fleece was a magical ram's skin of golden wool that once grew on the back of a creature that Hermes had used to save a young prince from a barbaric human sacrifice. The ram, possessed of golden wings, had flown over the Hellespont, the strait that separates Greece from Asia Minor, and had gotten the lad to sanctuary in far Colchis, a land so distant it seemed only a legend. When the great ram had eventually died, its skin was placed in the branches of a tree to be watched over by a dragon that never slept. Pelias pledged the contested throne to Jason on his happy return with the fleece in his possession. Jason was a young man itching for adventure and was cocky enough to believe in the impossible—he readily agreed to King Pelias's condition. But Colchis was so far that no one knew exactly where it was or what dangers would lie in wait, so Jason needed a stout ship and a crew of the sturdiest seamen and warriors he could find. The call went forth and the who's who of Greek heroism responded: Heracles the greatest hero of them all; Orpheus the singer; Peleus the father of Achilles and a pretty stalwart *hombre* in his own right; Lynceus with eyesight the eagles envied; Meleager, Zetes, and Calais the sons of the North Wind who had the winged feet to prove it; and so many more joined to fill the rowing benches of the vessel that would take them to lands unknown and experiences undreamt.

The crew was exemplary, but the ship and the ship maker were also of paramount importance to the undertaking. Argos the builder of the swiftest, strongest, and yet most graceful of sea craft in all the known world was conscripted for the task and the ship he built, the *Argo*, the finest vessel that a sailor had ever seen or had ever pierced the liquid folds of Poseidon's robe. It wasn't all Argos's doing, however, for the ship was built to the explicit specifications of the goddess Athena who had taken a liking to Jason—she seems to have always taken a shine for this sort of hardy boy—and within the stern was placed a beam that had the power to speak with Athena's own voice. Built, manned, and provisioned the *Argo* set off into the unknown waters of adventure. The isle of Lemnos was the Argonauts' first port o' call and quite the port it turned out to be.

I WANT You TO BE AN ARGONAUT!

Lemnos was populated entirely by women, who could be quite insistent that they be taken seriously and not for granted. The year before they pleaded with Aphrodite to make their men to turn toward them for comfort and not just to their slave girls. The goddess had rewarded them with an anger that left all the husbands and lovers, all males of a certain age, dead. Now the women found they needed men, not for the governance or the labor of the island, but for their pleasure and set upon the sailors. Heracles, who had wisely stayed aboard the *Argo,* quickly ascertained that if he did not go about separating the crew from the rewards of Lemnos, there would soon be no crew to venture to Colchis. With several fellow crewmen tucked under each arm at a time Heracles repopulated the *Argo.*

On to Samothrace and then the land of the Doliones where six-

armed monsters were quickly dispatched by the old club-swinger. An unfortunate case of mistaken identity left the hospitable king of the Doliones dead; the Argonauts grieved the traditional twelve days and were off to Thrace to leave sacrifices to Rhea, always good insurance. Heracles's great strength is proven too great for a normal oar and the Argonauts must make landfall once again so he can fashion a new one. While on shore, Heracles's squire, the very pretty Hylas, went off on his own to find a source of fresh water. He found it and more in the bargain. The local nymph spotted Hylas bending over the pool and she liked what she saw. Up goes her hands and down went Hylas to spend the rest of his days in a soggy love nest. Heracles was in great dismay, wondering what could have happened to his faithful servant and completely forgot the *Argo*, staying instead to hopelessly quest for the young man.

Still mourning the loss of their greatest

asset, the *Argo* sailed on to the Bithynia and to the killing of yet another king. This time the boxer Polydeuces fully intended to lay the ultimate knockout on the royal bully. But even a dust up with the newly kingless citizens of Bithynia could barely thwart their progress through the Bosporus and to see Phineus the seer, who was an unhappy resident of the western shore. Phineus was struck blind years before by a jealous Zeus who was convinced that the prophet was sharing much too much information. As was often the case with the gods, one punishment is simply not enough and Phineus was deviled daily by the Harpies. The scaly-tailed ladies would not let the blind man eat in peace; they stole his food and fouled his drink. When the Argonauts found him Phineus was starving and pledged to give them every assistance if they would rid him of the Harpies. With nary another word, the sons of the North Wind went to winged work and shooed the Harpies away to find new nests and other unfortunates to pester.

With a full belly for the first time in months, Phineus was eager to share all he knew. He informed the shipmates that ahead of them lay the *Symplegades*—the Clashing Rocks—and the only way to navigate the danger was to release a dove to distract the rocks. As the rocks pull apart, the men of the *Argo* must row as they have never rowed before. Jason and his crew followed Phineus's instruction down to the feather and with the aid of Athena they survived the geological wonder. Further landfalls and losses, but new recruits to fill the benches, kept the *Argo* plying the waves. Even the bronze-feathered birds of war that nested on the island of Ares could not stay their progress. The crew discovered that the birds, even these fierce hawks, were still birds and they didn't like noise one little bit. Swords banging away at shields kept the bronze feathers from falling their way.

A little more open sea and then the shores of Colchis lay dead ahead. Jason had the good fortune to not only have Athena in his corner but Hera as well. The queen of the gods must have been happy that here at last was a hero who couldn't claim Zeus as his *pater*. The two goddesses enlisted a third to aid their fair-haired boy; Aphrodite was conscripted to help in winning the fleece. Love was a weapon that had no equal, a weapon that no man or woman could withstand. Medea, the daughter of King Aeetes of Colchis, was the unwary victim of Eros's weapon, unleashed with all the other eating utensils at the feast welcoming the bold heroes to Colchis. Medea would prove to be a considerable ally of her new love, Jason, for not only was she a princess of the royal house but she was also a devotee of the goddess Hecate—in other words, a witch.

Jason did not beat around the bush with Aeetes; he got right to the fruit of his journey. The Golden Fleece would be a suitable exchange for the Argonauts' service. After all, where could any king find such a group of capable men, demigods or heroic warriors all, to do his biding? Jason's bargaining price did not have the desired effect, Aeetes exploded in anger and was ready to test his army's mettle against these foreign braggarts, but before he gave the bugle call of alarm he decided another less costly engagement would take care of the distasteful business. Residing in his stables, King Aeetes had two bulls as massive as elephants but with dispositions of the Furies. They were footed with sharp brass hooves and, to make the labor even more difficult, these monsters belched and blew fire from furnaces deep within their bellies. Jason need only to hitch the bulls to a plow and, after breaking the soil, plant an unusual seed, dragon's teeth, from which would grow men armed, dangerous, and ripe for a fight. He must, of course, defeat this vegetable army as soon as it sprang from furrows of the field. If Jason were willing and able to succeed at this bit of supernatural farming, he was more than welcome to the fleece. Confident in his skills, his crew's, and the aid of a particular love-struck witch, Jason assented to the challenge.

Having sacrificed to Hectate in a protection ritual conducted by Medea, Jason arrived at the pasture coated with a special salve that would repel even the flames of Helios. He was ready to hitch, plow, sow, and then reap what he had sown. He performed the grim agriculture of the day like he was born to farm the plains of Asphodel, where the warriors birthed of dragon's teeth were sent before the evening stretched its long shadows. Far from honoring the rules of the contest and in furious disbelief, Aeetes called out for the hands of the nighttime assassins to rid himself of these demanding Greeks. But Medea, who was privy to all councils, warned Jason of the skulking agents of death to come and in an act of further defiance took Jason to the sacred oak, using a potion to lull the dragon into an unshakeable slumber, and to the theft of the Golden Fleece.

They wasted not a moment to gain the *Argo*, rouse the crew, and row for the open sea as if all the armies of Colchis were after them, which they soon would be. The Argonauts followed Phineus's instruction and set a different course for home, one that involved following river courses and avoiding the Clashing Rocks and dangerous islands that dotted their earlier route. But they were at a decided disadvantage because the Colchians were more familiar with their local waters. Before the Greeks could enter the first river channel they were trapped by Medea's half-brother Absyrtus and the entire navy of the offended kingdom. But Medea was not one to docilely place her head into the noose. She planned a trap for her kin, and he would be the victim of Jason's waiting sword. Jason was appalled at such treachery, but he feared capture by the Colchians and now the wrath of his loving ally. The trap was sprung and the dismembered body of Absyrtus was tossed to the waves, slowing the disbelieving pursuers.

The Argonauts had escaped but with a despicable blood crime on their hands. Atonement was achieved by the ministrations of the witch Circe, but no one could banish the dread that now surrounded Medea. This was the new shipmate that walked the deck even as they sailed safely past the sirens, whose fatal song was drowned by Orpheus's even sweeter tune. Its dark visage shadowed the Argonauts' own faces as they swept through the pass of Scylla, a sea monster, and Charybdis, a whirlpool, with Hera's aid. It did not leave them even as they maneuvered out of the clutches of the Colchian navy. Jason and Medea's marriage sealed a truce between the thieves and their pursuers. And dread was ever the partner of this love they professed.

One last great adventure awaited as the *Argo* surfed closer to home. Hephaestus had created a robot, a huge bronze giant to guard the island of Crete. Perhaps the gods were taking pity on poor Crete after all the sad business of bull besotted queens and unnatural sons concluded. Talos was the giant's name and he unwaveringly patrolled the beaches on the lookout for unwanted immigrants. But the animated bronze statue was no match for the witch of Colchis.

120

She hypnotized him as he reached for boulders to break the hull of the *Argo,* and he stumbled, slashing his only vulnerable spot—a thinly covered heel. The massive heap of metal bled to death on the beach, no more a threat than a discarded stove.

At last, the Argonauts reached Iolcos. The Golden Fleece was placed in a nearby temple of Zeus, surprising considering Athena and Hera had been their protectors, and after some feasting the crew disbanded and headed off to their own homes and adventures. Yet even after the arduous task was completed and the fleece now graced Grecian shores, King Pelias was reluctant to give the throne to the true king of Iolcos. Ever the schemer, Medea concocted an elaborate plan to end the usurper's reign. With Pelias's daughters in tow, she killed an old ram and cut it into pieces. The pieces were thrown into a boiling cauldron and when the water cooled, out popped a pink and pearly lamb. The sisters agreed to the grisly experiment to rejuvenate their father, and to their surprise they only succeeded in making a horrible stew of dear old dad. Pelias was deposed, but instead of Jason ascending to the throne, he was shunned and driven out of Iolcos by a populace shocked by the crimes of his wife.

SOUP IS ON!

Here the story of Jason, and his wife Medea, descends completely and unalterably into tragedy. The couple with two sons in tow fled to Corinth, about the only city that would give them shelter after hearing the news of Medea's crimes. Unsurprisingly, Jason became more and more disenchanted and, frankly, fearful of his wife and consequently fonder of the king of Corinth, Creon, and especially fond of his daughter, Glauce. Medea learned his intentions, almost before Jason knew them—he wanted to dissolve their marriage and take vows anew with the princess. Medea was outraged and the King of Corinth, fearing what she might be capable of, ordered her and her boys to be expelled from the city. Jason attempted a sort of decency in all this sordid and sorry affair and went to Medea. He offered her gold and everything he could to protect what would soon be his former family. Medea, true to form, would have none of it, and instead was confirmed in her murderous ambition. After the nuptials, she anointed a robe with various poisons, a beautiful garment suited for a princess newly wed, and sent her boys to bear the gift to Glauce—for the casual observer a "let-bygones-be-bygones" gesture. As soon as the princess placed the garment on her shoulders and about her body the entire robe burst into flames and consumed the unwary bride.

The witch continued with

her rampage—justifying what she would do next as humane and the only way to protect the children. She killed her sons. Jason frantically beat at the door to protect the boys from the wrath of

King Creon, never suspecting what his former wife has already done. Still raging, Medea called on Helios, the founder of the royal house of Colchis, for assistance and her escape arrived—a flaming chariot drawn by dragons ascended the sky, allowing Medea and the two little corpses to leave Corinth and the Argonaut forever. Ever the wily, she settled in for a time with old Aegeus the king of Athens and had another son, Medus. She once again was forced to move on after trying to poison Theseus, Aegeus's long lost son. Further east she traveled with more schemes, mayhem, destruction to bring down on the heads of those unfortunate enough to be close to her.

Jason was devastated. No refuge could assuage his grief, guilt, the shattered wreck of his life. Eventually he returned to the shattered wreck that had been the triumph of his life, the *Argo*. The great ship sat beached and rotting in the sun and weather. Jason turned to the old ship for comfort and found that comfort for a time as he rested in its shade, but he was never to find the measure of peace he sought. The great arching stem of the ship, weakened by the age that befalls even the heroic, cracked and crashed on Jason's head. The hero was dead not by an enemy's mischief but by the proffered kindness of his greatest friend.

OEDIPUS. Hero? Antihero? Whatever description fits him best, Oedipus was, in some way the most popular man of myth for the ancients to write about. Homer, Hesiod certainly, but even more certainly he occupies the very heart of the Greek tragedians. Aeschylus, Euripides, and especially Sophocles singled out the tragic tale of the man to be set in drama. Laius and Jocasta were the rulers of Thebes but not the entirely happy rulers of their own bedchamber. Laius for a grave infraction (abduction of another king's son) had been given a terrible prophecy—he would die by the hand of his own son. Consequently, he decided not to make any sons, but Jocasta did not marry to remain celibate and succeeded in tricking the king into her bed to enjoy her appealing charms. A son was born and, as in many a fairy tale, the solution was to have a servant place the infant on a far hillside where he would be wolf chow in no time. As insurance in this grim matter, Laius had a spike driven through the baby's feet so he could not possibly escape. But as it happens in these tales the servant took sympathy on the poor newborn and newly crippled lad, and he found a kind Corinthian shepherd to pass him to. The shepherd removed the horrible nail, named the boy Oedipus, which means "disfigured feet," and carried him to the childless rulers of Corinth, Polybus and Merope, who were overjoyed to have a son to love. Oedipus grew up in the court of Corinth, never suspecting his true parentage until, at a party, a drunken lout blurted out that Oedipus was no true son of the king. What's a boy to do? He hiked to Delphi and the oracle, of course. The Oracle gave him a terrible reading—Oedipus would kill his father and marry his own mother! Disgusted, angered, saddened, Oedipus departed from Delphi with a solemn pledge never to return to Corinth.

So off to Thebes he traveled. At a crossroads, always a fateful place, he encountered an incredibly disagreeable man in a chariot. The man ordered him to step aside in a most unpleasant way. A fight commenced and both the man and his charioteer finished it by lying dead at young Oedipus's feet. Oedipus carried on leaving the two men behind him.

More adventures awaited him before his feet took him to Thebes. A short distance from the city a monster stood guard plaguing all travelers with riddles. It wasn't bad humor that killed those who could not answer, but the teeth of the fearsome and strangely attractive Sphinx. The Sphinx with her beautiful face and torso that was seamlessly attached to the winged body of a lion made a quick meal of everyone afflicted with slow wits. Thus far no one was able to answer her riddle and all had become Sphinx food. Oedipus boldly marched up to she who would have him for lunch. And in a voice both musical and menacing the monster asked her question: "What walks on four legs in the morning, two at noontime, and three in the evening?" Our hero was smart and ready and readily he answered: "A man, because he walks on four as a baby in the morning of his life, two as an adult in the middle, and three when using a cane as an elder." The Sphinx could not believe her ears. She shuddered. She quaked. And in an act of shame at being bested, she killed herself on the spot.

Oedipus entered the city as a savior! The Thebans were overjoyed at their deliverance from the dread riddler and, as it so happened, the queen was newly widowed and in need of a new consort. Oedipus could easily see that Queen Jocasta might be a little older than him, but she was still a most desirable woman. Wedding bells soon rang out and everyone settled into a happy and prosperous time. Fifteen years went quickly by and Oedipus and Jocasta were the proud parents of a new brood. Life had been good, until suddenly and inexplicably things soured in Thebes. Plagues, pestilence, and famine all struck the city as if Moses had come to town, but there was no clear cause. Tiresias, the itinerant prophet, arrived shortly thereafter and was pressed into "seervice." Tiresias intoned that Thebes was suffering from a sort of time-activated fate brought on by the murder of the former king and the murderer was his own son. Son? Those who knew anything about royal offspring knew that the child had been dispatched as an infant. The investigation turned to the servant who had been ordered to leave the lad for the wolves. He admitted he could not bring himself to abandon the child on the hillside and had instead passed him to a Corinthian shepherd. The story unwound eventually to its dreadful conclusion: Oedipus was the father-murdering and consequently mother-marrying son!

This news was too horrifying for the couple in question. Jocasta hanged herself and Oedipus, in an act of remorse and profound disgust, blinded himself and committed himself to self-imposed exile. Again he wandered in fear of himself. His daughter Antigone joined Oedipus on his stumbling way. His other daughter, loyal and loving Ismene, remained in Thebes, while his sons, Eteocles and Polynices, not only rejected their father but conspired against Jocasta'a brother Creon who had assumed leadership of the city. The blind outcast at last came to the Athenian city of Colonus and was given sanctuary by King Theseus, no stranger to troubles himself. But the grieving Oedipus is given no relief because the politics of Thebes will know no relief. His sons conspired and Polynices raised an army to storm their city and gain control by bloodshed. Oedipus cursed them for the faithless and power hungry louts they were, but they went right ahead with their plan to wage war against those that they hoped to rule.

126

It was too much for Oedipus. He prayed and his prayers were answered in the form of black cloud that writhed internally with storm and thunder. The cloud descended and Oedipus walked forward into the embracing darkness never to walk the geography of earth again. There was a general mourning, if not sympathy, for the blinded sufferer, for what man could know what blind fate could offer them in the way of a future? Antigone returned to Thebes in time to suffer the next round of family misfortune. Her brothers lead their army to the walls and were rebuffed and defeated. Both were killed but Polynices body, so close to the bulwarks, was left unattended, dishonored in the dust. Even though Antigone was angry with her brother, his passing needed to be acknowledged and a proper funeral conducted. Creon, however, had a different point of view and chose to let the remains of the traitor rot where it fell as a warning to all would-be insurrectionists. Creon, king of Thebes and now without opposition, considered the matter closed. Antigone would not allow yet another desecration to be forced upon her family. Against the order of the king, she went out of the city and gathered the mortal remains of her brother and took them to entombment with the proper rites. In despair she joined Polynices in the tomb.

Tiresias, always a man to be reckoned with, arrived in Thebes to warn Creon against his rash actions. The curse on the house of Thebes would not end with this but continue on with him unless he took immediate action to allay it. Creon tried but was too late; Antigone had hanged herself in the tomb. Thebes's curse was not lifted. The royal house was further doomed. We remember Oedipus not for his defeating a monster but for the monster he released unwittingly from within himself. Now that is complex.

HERACLES. The greatest hero of them all. He who won a thousand battles. He who suffered a thousand tragedies. He whose name lives on and on and of all the heroes of ancient Greece really does not need an introduction, but introduce him I will. Even though a living man or men may have inspired his exploits, it's with the mythological Heracles that we will travel. Zeus, ever on the lookout for desirable human women, was inspired by the beautiful Alcmene, but in a rare display of patience Zeus waited to have his way with her until after her husband Amphitryon had gone off to war in defense of his native Thebes. Once the warrior was safely occupied, Zeus in the guise of her husband visited Alcmene, and Heracles and his twin Iphicles were conceived. The proud parents may have put two and two together right then and there but probably remained blissfully ignorant of the babies' true parentage until Zeus kidnapped baby Heracles. Safe in papa's arms he was carried to Olympus and placed at the breast of Hera while she slumbered. Discovering the unknown infant at her breast, Hera pushed him away and her breast gushed into the heavens what would from then on be known as the Milky Way (an alternative version of this story is Phaeton's bumbling at the reins of Helios's chariot was to blame for this celestial phenomenon). Zeus was tickled with his bit of chicanery for even though he had just made Heracles a lifelong enemy of the queen of the gods, even if Heracles actually means "glory of Hera," he had also assured his son of becoming immortal. Hera was always one to cry over a little spilled milk, and she plotted revenge on the infant Heracles.

She sent two venomous serpents into the nursery of the sleeping boys. They slithered into the babies' crib and the exact moment they raised to strike, the chubby little fists of Heracles closed about their throats. The snakes drank their own venom that day. When the cries of Iphicles brought parents, nursemaids, and the entire household into the children's room, all saw the heroic act of this remarkable bundle. This kid was cut from a different cloth than the wise, sensitive Iphicles.

Amphitryon was amazed and suitably proud of his offspring's ability to choke the life out of a couple of scaly intruders, but mainly he was amazed. He consulted with Tiresias the blind prophet about his child's remarkable abilities. Tiresias was a man who was possessed of his own remarkable abilities. Once when out walking he came across two serpents tangled in a love knot in the middle of the path. The snakes were not content to just finish their business but, in a state of belligerent agitation, attacked Tiresias. In his defense the man killed the female serpent and was immediately given a sex change—Tiresias to, let's say, Tiresia. Years later while out wandering the same path, Tiresia once again stumbled upon two snakes mating in the center of the footpath and once again they turned to strike at the "lady" who had disturbed them in this moment of public intimacy. This time in defending herself from the venomous jaws Tiresia killed the male snake and was instantly returned to maleness. Unique among humans, Tiresias knew what it was like to have been both male and female.

This unique transgenderal experience made Tiresias the perfect candidate to resolve a dispute between Zeus and Hera. The argument was over who enjoyed the sex act more, male or female? Each of the divines was contending that the opposite gender was the greater recipient of pleasure. Tiresias was able to respond with complete honesty that the female enjoyed the pleasure. Hera in yet another display of her gentle spirit struck Tiresias blind. Zeus felt bad for the honest fellow and certainly did not mind being corrected, so he rewarded Tiresias with the gift of prophecy and a very long life. So to Amphitryon's question about young Heracles's truly surprising nature, Tiresias was able to respond that not only was the boy gifted with super human strength among other attributes but he also was not Amphitryon's natural born son. Heracles's father was of divine origin and he was particularly blessed with lightning powers.

Amphitryon got the message and decided to train up the child in all the various and sundry arts of peace and war that would be necessary for an extraordinary career. Amphitryon learned that even as a child the boy Heracles had a difficult and frightening temper. While at a music lesson the young buck flew into a rage brought on by the instructor's tap with a lyre and inadvertently killed the teacher. Amphitryon dispatched Heracles to the farms to try his hand at agricultural labor.

Heracles loved the work and grew even stronger into young adulthood. From farmer to heroic adventurer did not take a great deal of transition, and it was no time before Heracles was out doing what heroes are meant to do. He fought and killed the lion of Mount Kithairon after the beast had ravaged the countryside and made all the local villagers' lives a living hell. He took the skin of the feline and used it as his emblematic garment with the lion's hollowed head resting over his like a hood and the rest of the trophy hanging from his shoulders in a cape-like manner. Thus robed he not only played the part of the hero but looked like it, too. While Heracles was out in the hills taking care of the beast, danger came to the gates of Thebes. King Orchomenus, a longtime enemy of the city and its king, Creon, attacked. Heracles first stripped the temples of all the weapons that had been placed in them as tribute and armed every available Theban. Then, in a strategic stroke of genius, he dammed the river Cephissus and flooded the entirety of Orchomenus's crops. Needless to say, the invaders were turned back and Heracles was the "fair-haired boy" of Thebes. Creon showered Heracles with gifts and even gave him his own daughter Megara to wed. Almost as fast as they could conceive children Megara gave birth to them. In no time Heracles was the proud papa of eight little Heracloids. It looked as if things would become quite domesticated for Heracles with his newfound prosperity and familial bliss. But Hera had other plans for the strongman, heart-wrenching plans.

DAM IT!

Hera sent madness to inhabit the soul of the innocent Heracles. In his condition he took up the great club that had become his weapon of choice and in a jaw-slavering rage attacked his beloved nephew Iolas. Iolas managed to escape but six of Heracles's own children were not so lucky. With an even greater cruelty Hera restored Heracles to sanity and the terrible realization of what he had done. Immediately, Heracles isolated himself from all human contact in a dread fear of all he had done and all he might do. He was eventually persuaded to perform purification rituals and to travel to Delphi and ask the oracle there what he might do to atone for his horrendous crimes. The oracle sent him on to Argos and into the servitude of King Eurystheus. It was these twelve labors assigned to him by the king that turned Heracles into the hero of this age and every other age to follow.

1. *The Nemean Lion* terrorized the city and country of Nemea. It was a huge and seemingly invincible beast. Heracles was sent by Eurystheus to kill this cat first as it would be a quite good opening act for the well-known lion slayer. The lion proved to be more of a match than his brethren on Mount Kithairon. This creature seemed to possess a skin that was completely impenetrable by any weapon. Once again Heracles used his brains as well as his muscle, trapped the monster in his lair, and clubbed him into submission, finally choking him as the *coup de gras*. The skin he presented to King Eurystheus was the proof of his conquest.

2. *The Hydra of Lerna* lived in a swamp not far from the city of Argos. It was a reptilian offspring of the Titan Typhon and had been placed in the environs by Hera to devil her hated stepchild. Heracles conscripted his nephew Iolas to accompany him on this venture into the dank bogs. It took no great time to locate the lair of the Hydra; carnage decorated its whereabouts like signposts. When they arrived, the creature seemed to have no interest in coming out to play even after Heracles fired a couple of flaming arrows through the cave mouth. Hera couldn't resist adding yet another obstacle and sent a huge and ill-tempered crab in to harry Heracles's legs. Despite its shell the crab didn't last long under the repeated hammering of Heracles's club, just long enough to coax the Hydra into action. From each of its nine heads the Hydra exhaled a noxious breath, so Heracles got to work with his sword while holding his breath. Even without being completely oxygenated Heracles could easily see that his deadly slicing and dicing only made matters worse; when one head was struck off, two more grew in its place. Iolas proved invaluable aid as he took a torch and underneath the snapping jaws he would scrabble to cauterize the decapitated necks and stop further regeneration. The ninth head proved particularly stubborn, as it was immortal and not about to succumb to death even when severed. Heracles succeeded in planting the nasty hissing thing so deep no treasure seeker would ever come across it. He then dipped his arrows in its poisonous blood, and Iolas and Heracles called it a day well spent.

3. *The Erymanthian Boar* was placed next on the list and Heracles tracked it across the snow-covered mountains of Mount Erymanthus until the pig was trapped in the deep snow and could run no more. Heracles played cowboy by jumping atop its heaving back until he could chain the stamping legs together. In one mighty heave, he switched positions with the mighty porker, threw it atop his back, and proceeded back to Argos to present his live specimen. King Eurystheus proved himself to be better at selecting labors than taking part in them for he hid in a jar trembling until the boar was taken far away.

4. *The Ceryneian Hind* was a beautiful creature and a wonderful break from the snorting, belching monsters Heracles was sent to take care of heretofore. In fact, he was under a strict proviso not to harm the golden-horned, brazen-hoofed, beloved pet of Artemis in any way. But some tasks only sound easy. Heracles, who could have dispatched the beast in moments, spent a year chasing it until finally the poor creature dropped in exhaustion. Finally, the Hind could rest on Heracles's shoulders as he returned with it to Argos before its sweet release back into the wilds.

5. *The Stymphalian Birds* were thousands of winged nuisances that plagued the area of Lake Stymphalus in Arcadia. They cried and called endlessly, driving even the deaf to madness. They pillaged the local farms, and their droppings fouled the lake and everything unfortunate enough to be beneath them. Heracles was, as usual, stymied by the agencies of Hera but on this adventure he was also aided by the good agency of Athena. The goddess persuaded Hephaestus to manufacture a great bronze rattle, a singularly peculiar weapon for the hero but a most effective one. Heracles shook the rattle and the crashing, bashing, teeth-chattering, and peace-shattering noise drove the birds off, never to be seen or heard from ever again.

6. *The Augean Stables* were King Eurystheus's way of enabling Heracles to use his long-dormant farm skills. Augeas was a king that didn't just have a herd of cattle or a flock of sheep; he had an army of animals that made his land of Elis look like the Amarillo, Texas, of the ancient world. He had also been granted a dispensation from the gods that ensured that his animals would never suffer from any disease, so why clean? The stables and barns of Augeas were the filthiest place on the face of a fairly untidy world. And the flies that swarmed away from this fabled kingdom of cow pies and horse apples spread all the diseases from which his animals were immune. Heracles, agriculturist and engineer, set to work on his bold plan. With shovel in hand he changed the course of the river Alpheus and its diverted waters churned and splashed through the stables and back to the river's regular channel, finally depositing all the accumulated acres of pooh into the sea. King Eurystheus accepted Heracles's word that the stables were clean.

8. _The Horses of Diomedes_ were a terrifying team of four huge stamping, kicking equines that pulled the chariot of the king. King Diomedes, a son of Ares, was a regular chip off the old block; the preferred cuisine of the horses was human flesh. Travelers were warned about visiting Thrace for they often found ac-commodations in the bellies of Diomedes's team. Heracles, al-ways the farmhand, was ready for the challenge and marched right into the stables and tethered the ponies on a single halter. Diomedes heard the commotion and quickly rushed in with his troops to stop the theft. Clubbed into unconsciousness by our hero, Diomedes felt nothing as his dis-loyal horses enjoyed a meal of him. Upon digesting the repro-bate they immediately became docile—not a method recom-mended by horse whisperers.

7. _The Cretan Bull_ may or may not have been the fellow that cuck-olded King Minos, but he was more than happy to be rid of it in any case. Heracles corralled the beast and brought it home to Argos and King Eurystheus. The king was as happy to see the bull as he was the boar and promptly had it released. Where once he had turned Crete into the proverbial china shop, he now had his way with Argos. Eventually, the brute was driven out to Marathon and later taken care of by Theseus.

9. *The Girdle of Hippolyta* was not a superhuman foundation garment owned by the queen of the Amazons but rather a belt given to the warrior women by their benefactress Hera. The Amazons had a reputation for ferocity that rivaled almost any of the monsters on the strongman's "to do" list. These women reputedly went so far as to sever their left breasts in order to shoot their bows more accurately and they certainly would not sit idly by as a man trespassed in their kingdom to filch such a sacred relic. Heracles was assisted in this undertaking by his friend Theseus and the two of them made a fairly handy work of the theft. Hell to pay came later when the Amazons invaded Athens in revenge, but in a rare happy ending in Greek mythology, Theseus and Hippolyta were later wed thus ending all international hostilities and any domestic hostilities seemed to have been negligible.

10. *The Cattle of Geryon* were beautiful red bovines coveted by everyone including Eurystheus. Heracles was ordered to bring the cattle back to Argos. Geryon himself was a monster, a descendent of Medusa and Poseidon; he could be described as either a man with one head and three bodies or one body and three heads. In any case, this strange triplet lived as far west as anyone in the known world. For the sea voyage, Helios lent Heracles a huge golden cup to use and, for such an ungainly seagoing vessel, it made good time across the Mediterranean. In fact, Heracles was so pleased when he reached his destination he erected a geologic monument that was known for centuries as the pillars of Heracles but now goes by the monikers of the Rock of Gibraltar and the Mountain of Ceuta on the African side. Of course, Geryon wasn't about to give up his cattle willingly, so Heracles proceeded to kill his herder, his two-headed watchdog Orthrus, and the oddly formed cattleman himself. Heracles loaded the cattle into the wine cup, and with his lion skin under full sail, he made Argos in no time. Eurystheus was more than pleased with his new shining red herd, and Helios was happy to get his cup back, but he washed it repeatedly before he drank from it again.

11. *The Theft of Cerberus*, the three-headed guard dog of Hades, seemed to be the labor that would put an end to Heracles once and for all. Eurystheus was happy for the gift of Geryon's cattle but he was ready to be rid of the gifter. Heracles could not set off to the underworld until he knew where it was, and Hermes the psychopomp was more than happy to be his guide. Athena also pledged assistance once Heracles entered the realm of the dead.

Heracles needed no help in bullying Charon, who was the bully of souls, into manning the oars across the river Styx. But Hades was a different matter for he was none too keen on letting the hero kidnap his triple-headed pup. A fight ensued and Hades was bested by Heracles, who agreed to let Cerberus be taken on the condition that no weapon would be used in the capturing. Heracles was quite the master of the leash and had the dog eating out of his hand in no time. Somewhere in the dreaded labyrinth of the underworld Heracles discovered his friend and cohort Theseus languishing in the Chair of Forgetfulness, and it took all his strength to separate the Minotaur-slayer from the seat. Athena happily did the rowing back across the river as Charon found it advantageous to absent himself from his boat until Heracles was safely back in the land of the living. Upon entering the palace of Eurystheus with his new pet, Heracles was not surprised to find the absence of greetings. Eurystheus once again commanded from his jar until Cerberus was returned to his rightful owner.

138

12. *The Golden Apples of the Hesperides* were the fruit of a very special tree that grew in Hera's gardens in the far west. The daughters of the Titan Atlas, the so-called Hesperides, tended the lush precinct. Atlas himself stood on a mountain close by in punishment for warring against the Olympians. On his broad shoulders he was doomed to forever hold the vault of heaven. Finding the garden was another problem to beset Heracles with for its whereabouts were unknown to mortals (even though Heracles had suckled at Hera's breast and that nourishment made immortality possible his status was still a little nebulous). Thrashing old sea god Nereus led him to the burdened Atlas. The Titan consented to help Heracles in this quest if first Heracles would help him.

HOW DO YOU LIKE DEM APPLES?

The apples themselves could only be plucked by immortal hands and that meant Atlas would have to do the picking, but the tree was guarded by a dragon of which anyone, god or mortal, would be terrified—Heracles had to first kill off the lizard. This posed no problem for the hero as a couple of well-placed arrows in the scaly hide sent the Hydra's venom coursing through the monster's bloodstream. Of course, Atlas couldn't go fetch the apples and carry the sky at the same time, so assistance was required. Heracles readily took the weight of the heavens onto his shoulders and Atlas went off on his fruit-picking mission. The Titan returned with the apples but in the interim had decided to extend his brief vacation—he would take the apples to Eurystheus and Heracles could remain holding up the old workload. Heracles admitted that he had been had fair and square, but he begged one final concession from Atlas. As he hadn't expected to be doing this arduous task for more than a few moments, he hadn't taken the time to comfortably adjust his lion robe on his shoulders.

Would Atlas be a pal and take the sky for a few minutes while Heracles did his adjustment? In the spirit of fair play, Atlas assented and in no time the old switcheroo had been achieved and Heracles, with apples in hand, was headed back to Argos, and the finishing of his twelfth and final labor. On the journey home, Heracles ran into the giant Antaeus and needless to say wrestling ensued. Heracles just couldn't get the better of his opponent until he noticed each time Antaeus's feet were in contact with terra firma he seemed to come back with renewed strength. Because the big bully was a child of Gaea the earth, being in touch with mommy added power to the son. Discerning this replenishing source, Heracles lifted Antaeus into the air and held him there until he had squeezed the life out of him. After that the road to Argos was a breeze. But when all was said and done Eurystheus didn't really like the apples because they might incur the wrath of Hera, so he promptly passed them on to Athena and she restored them to the garden.

Heracles for his part was a free man once again and was happy to leave Argos in his metaphorical rearview mirror forever. Heracles was back in the world of his own choosing. He and Megara separated with such a tragedy forever between them, and Heracles's nephew Iolas took her as his wife. The strong man wandered a bit, finding various ways to get in trouble and then redeeming himself. He defenestrated a guest in a moment of white-hot anger; he got himself in a punching match with Apollo; he even went to war with Troy long before the fabled Trojan wars. Heracles even found himself indentured to yet another ruler after his temper flared in the wrong direction. This time it was a pleasant servitude bonded to King Omphale of Lydia. His tasks under the queen resulted in three sons.

Years of unsettled adventure, war, and general carousing left Heracles in need of a life a little more predictable, a little less chaotic, and with an element of blissful boredom. In Aetolia he met, fought for, and wed the princess Deianara. Heracles was content to spend the rest of his days in happy domesticity but the pesky Fates had other plans in mind. While traveling, the couple came to a deep and treacherous river with no safe way of crossing. A centaur named Nessus happened to overhear the spouses' discussion and graciously offered his services. Deianara could climb upon his back and he would have her across the river in no time—and once across the river, "have her" he tried. If it hadn't been for Heracles's quick club, his new wife would have been raped by the duplicitous centaur. As Nessus lay dying he called Deianara to him. He told her how mortally sorry he was for his attempted crime and he wanted to give her a gift in order to atone for it. If she would collect a quantity of his blood and the seed he spilled on the ground and mix it together she would have a powerful antidote for her hero's future wandering eye. All that needed to be done was to spread it in a shirt and when he put it on he would return to her never to leave again.

Deianara knew Heracles loved her but she was also aware that a celebrated man such as he was would have ample opportunities to seek fulfillment outside the bonds of their marriage. She preserved the mixture in a jar and waited. Of course, Heracles could never just become a househusband content to ride the couch and grow fat on olives and feta, so it wasn't long before he found a war that needed his participation.

I CALL IT MEDICINE.

And it was no time before he sent a captive home to Deianara, a beautiful young princess named Iole. It took even less time for that escapee from Pandora's box, jealousy, to find its way to Deianara's door and into her heart. A fresh new tunic of the finest linen was anointed with Nessus's "antidote" and sent to Heracles. Heracles was overjoyed at the gift from his dear wife and hesitated not a moment in taking off his quite used shirt and throwing on his comfortable new tunic. Comfort transformed to agony in an instant when Heracles was convulsed in burning pain. Nessus had his revenge with a concoction that proved to be a horrendous poison without an antidote.

Heracles knew that end was near and summoned his son Hyllus and devoted nephew Iolas to build a funeral pyre on Mount Oeta and to transport him there. Heracles placed atop the pyre and neither Iolas nor Hyllus could bring themselves to set it alight. A boy passing by obeyed the suffering hero and the flames shot up around him. Zeus seeing his son in such agony could bear no more and sent a lightning bolt to reduce the pyre and all it consumed to ashes, taking the still living Heracles to Olympus and true unfailing godhood. The inconsolable Deianara took her own life. Heracles at long last was able to reconcile with his stepmother, and Hera accepted the club-swinger as a true son. Heracles even married her daughter Hebe. The greatest hero that earth would ever know was gone from the earth but the gods put his adventures for all to see forever in the night sky. There is the lion, the crab, the dragon, the Hydra, and Heracles himself swinging his great club until the end of time. Look to the stars and do Heracles honor.

3. The Epics of Homer

Sing to me, oh, goddess… Ah, with those words begins the great epics of a blind poet who just might be as mythological as the tales he tells. These tales were part of a great oracular tradition that was coming to an end when they were finally set down for the reader and not the listener to enjoy. Who knows how many variations in the tellings there might have been when one after another variously gifted performers strummed their lyres and sang these doings of great heroes from ancient days. And then all the different voices congealed into one and the one became attached to "Homer." Homer we know very little about: he was blind, he was a bard, he was illiterate and gave great dictation, and he probably never existed. Whoever it may have been that took pen to parchment, whether they were named Homer or even Jethro, left us with a bifurcated tale of adventure, war, greed, capricious gods, and terribly flawed heroes like none that had ever appeared before. The *Iliad* and the *Odyssey* are multileveled, multifaceted stories that at their very core have a prime theme, a different but related theme in each. In the *Iliad*, the hero, Achilles, searches for some honor and meaning in a war that has ground on for almost a decade and in the *Odyssey* the hero, Odysseus, struggles to return to his home. Both themes would appear over and over in the literature that would follow these epics. Both themes will continue to be prime concerns in all the literature to come. Just something about human existence that we still have to work out I guess. Both epics are comprised of twenty-four books each and neither starts at the beginning of their story. They digress, meander, and are punctuated with both boredom and bombast. Other authors have stepped in to fill the gaps and to add what might be missing to tell the whole story. Whatever the flaws inherent in these twenty-five hundred year old epics to our modern eyes, whatever disagreements live within the words, whatever… these are the still some of the greatest works of literature ever set by human hand on pages to be read and read and read. This author will try to simply put them down chronologically and with some information added to tell the full story.

THE *ILIAD*. The story begins nine years or more into the Trojan War. Zeus, the philanderer in chief, lusted after a beautiful queen named Leda. In an act of poetic transformation, the king of the gods appeared to the object of his desire in the guise of a swan. Leda, having some strange, if not unnatural, affection for large birds, had sex with the swan. Some months later she laid an egg that cracked to reveal a boy, Pollux, and a girl, Helen (another boy, Castor, was birthed the old fashioned way). But what a girl Helen was! She grew into a beauty never before seen in humankind. She was loved, wooed, kidnapped, and envied by gods and men. Eventually, Helen

was given in marriage to Menelaus, the king of Sparta, but while all of this transpired other things were afoot: a golden apple inscribed with the appellation that it was to be gifted to only the "fairest" had been tossed by the uninvited Eris, goddess of discord, into a prominent wedding feast, such a tony affair that the deities were in attendance. The precious fruit caused an uproar and was resolved by holding a beauty contest to be judged by a young prince of Troy named Paris.

No matter how beautiful the contestants were, and these were pretty good-looking goddesses, Hera, Athena, and Aphrodite, each one was reduced to trickery to win the battle. Aphrodite secured the apple by a pledge to supply Paris with the most beautiful woman in the world. Of course, that woman happened to be Helen and she happened to be married, a mere technicality for the two young lovers, as they quickly became, and they eloped to Troy in no time. Menelaus and his brother Agamemnon the king of Argos bullied, cajoled, and called in favors to create an army of all the Greeks and thus Helen "was the face that launched a thousand ships." And all those ships were headed to Troy to get Menelaus's wayward wife back.

So we rush those nine years into the future and the war drags on. Tensions had risen to dangerous levels in the Greek army and the pressure cookers in breastplates began to blow up. Agamemnon had taken captive a young girl named Chryseis, daughter of a priest of Apollo, and he didn't want to give her up. Apollo sent a plague of big, ugly biting flies to beset the Greeks, and fly-bitten Agamemnon at last relented, but everybody had to compensate him for his loss. Achilles was ordered to give his beautiful captive, Briseis, up to the king. Achilles did not like this imperious command, but he reluctantly submitted to the will of a higher authority. He also prayed to Zeus to help the Trojans so the Greeks (i.e., Agamemnon) would see how much they need Achilles. So much for the vaunted honor of heroes.

With just this short visit to the war one can see the influence of the gods on the proceedings. The gods were never ones to shy away from a good, or even bad, fight and this world war needed their intimate attention. Some of the divinities picked a side and stayed with them—Athena and Hera were definitely Greek supporters. Aphrodite (who was instrumental in causing the mess in the first place), Apollo, and Ares were firmly within the walls of Troy, and Zeus was mainly in the camp of the Greeks. The gods not only offered their godly support but also took an active role in the fighting. Aphrodite and Ares were even injured in battle. Is it any wonder the war took so long to fight when venality, both divine and human, was truly what the muses seemed to be singing about?

Trying a ploy to gauge his fighters' commitment to the fight and thinking he would renew that stalwart commitment, Agamemnon announced that it was time to pack up and hit the beach for home. The Greeks headed for the ships and Agamemnon was crushed— just kidding, just kidding! Drop your suitcases and grab your swords! The war continued, but without the able accompaniment of Achilles, who had decided to sit this dance out and let them all step on each other's toes. A brief word about the Greeks' invincible hero, or mostly invincible: Achilles was the son of Peleus the former Argonaut and Thetis, a nymph, and one of Zeus's beloveds. Thetis, in an act that any mother could understand, had assured her baby boy's invulnerability by dipping the said infant into the river Styx. By this baptism Achilles's skin became his armor—except there was one technicality. With the ability to dip him only once and to minimize any weak spots, Thetis had taken a firm grip on Achilles's heel to complete the immersion. What difference could a pregnable heel make when the rest of you is impregnable?

JK! JK! EVERYBODY BACK UP THE BEACH!

146

While Achilles stewed in his juices, the war continued to provide more meat for the vultures. Paris, an active participant in the war's cause, challenged any Greek leader to step out of the ranks and meet him in mortal combat. Menelaus, who had more than a bone to pick with his young cuckold, gladly accepted the challenge. Combat ensued and much to his dismay, things did not go well for Paris.

Only the goddess of love, whisking Paris away could save him from a good drubbing. Just itching to scratch Paris's head off with his sword, Menelaus was less than pleased. Unlike modern impersonal warfare, Homer's recounting of the Trojan war often resembled the bout card of professional wrestling—Hector, brother of Paris and Troy's greatest warrior, would meet the mighty Ajax in a no-holds-barred match before the walls of Troy (these heavyweight bad-boys fought to a draw and exchanged gifts afterword, retaining the Hellenic world's status as a civilized locale).

Hand-to-hand combat was fought by individual warriors—Diomedes, Idomeneus, and old King Nestor battling for the Greeks and Glaucus, Sarpedon, and Dolon weighing in for the Trojans. Blood and treachery were dispensed in equal measure. At Zeus's insistence, the gods bowed off the actual battlefield, but held an advisory role—until, of course, they could no longer resist swinging a sword or driving a chariot into the ranks of the opposing contestants. But not surprisingly, the real war was being fought off the battlefield and in the tents of the Greek allies. Agamemnon was ever the power-hungry leader trying to bend the wills of these unruly petty kings of Greece to his dominant, arrogant, and insecure will. For the most part he managed to bully enough of them to keep the war going—nine years represented a lot of will bending—but one petulant warrior refrained from being twisted into submission.

Achilles lounged around his digs, strummed his lyre, drank wine, and continued in his snit. He did not go home, but he did not don his breastplate and greaves either. His beloved nephew, Patroclus, had an idea. Achilles could let him borrow his idle armor and lead Achilles' troops, the Myrmidons (these fellows were the descendents of the people of Achilles's island of Aegina, and their ancestors had been transformed into humans from ants after Hera, in a hissy fit, had killed all the original inhabitants) and then win the battle while Achilles still held his fast from battle in his tent. Patroclus was persistent and succeeded in getting his way. Everything went swimmingly until Apollo intervened—so much for Zeus's hands-off policy—stunned the boy, and left him for Hector to finish. Hector stripped the corpse and just couldn't wait to parade about in Achilles's armor.

Achilles was a wreck. He loved the boy and now all he could do was mourn him after he managed, with Athena's aid, to retrieve the battered and broken body. Achilles was ready to return to the battle and return he did, splitting the Trojan army down the center and splitting many a Trojan helmet and skull along the way. Apollo was busy urging the Trojans on but no one it seemed could stand before the reaping sword of the grieving Greek hero. And then gods or no gods, Achilles found Hector and dispatched him to Hades. Death was not enough vengeance for Achilles; dishonor was to follow. Achilles pierced Hector's feet and tied them to his chariot and dragged the still warm body across the gravel of the battlefield back to the Greek encampment. Now at last Achilles felt that he could put Patroclus to rest. After he dreamt a tender dream of his departed nephew in which Patroclus told him that they would soon be reunited, Achilles ignited the byre and then entombed the cold ashes. But between vows to turn Hector's body into dog food and dragging it around Patroclus's tomb, Achilles would not be consoled. Nor would Hector's body be consumed for it miraculously still retained a freshness not normal for a much-abused corpse.

And still the gods wrangled on Olympus and would not let men settle their own differences. Finally, after much bitterness and dispute among his peers, Zeus accepted the prayer of King Priam, the father of dead Hector, to be allowed to retrieve the corpse of his son. Priam with Hermes as his guide and in the disguise of a Myrmidon entered the Greek encampment and eventually the tent of Achilles. He pled his case, the tears of a saddened weary old man beaten to the ground by war, and the personal tragedy of Hector's death. Achilles was moved and allowed Priam to gather the cold body of his son and return to Troy. A great funeral was conducted within the walls of the city, the flames climbed to lick the underside of the heavens, and the mortal remains of Hector were consigned back to the earth.

And so ends the *Iliad.* The conscientious reader might ask what happened next. Well, the end to the war with Troy can be found tucked in various nooks and crannies of the *Odyssey* and some other sources but in the interest of continuity we will carry on. As it was prophesized by his departed cousin, Achilles's tenure in this mortal realm was to be short. Not long after the twin funeral pyres had cooled to their last embers, Paris, who had caused this terrible conflict and had yet to prove his worth on the battlefield, fired an arrow straight with the guidance of Apollo's hand into the one vulnerable spot on the body of Greece's great hero, the right heel. Down the mighty Achilles fell and writhed in agony until he died. Hector was avenged.

And still the war continued and might still continue to this day if it had not been for a new Greek hero, one who, although a capable swinger of the sword, distinguished himself much more in the battlefields of the wits, clever Odysseus. Odysseus was king of the isle of Ithaca and he was most definitely a homeboy who wanted nothing more than to be left alone to raise his family and tend his vineyards in peace. But alliances were alliances and when Agamemnon came recruiting to raise his war machine bound for Troy, he came knocking at Odysseus's door. In a moment of inspiration Odysseus feigned madness, and it was a very good performance even to setting his plow to furrow the rocky and salt saturated beach. There being other clever fellows in the Greek army, one in true Solomonic fashion placed the "madman's" infant son Telemachus in the path of the sharp farm implement and caught Odysseus in his ruse when he turned the plow away.

The devoted father was soon sailing with his troops for Troy. All the while he prayed, hoped, and schemed to end this curse of war so he could return to his home. Now Odysseus had his chance and his greatest scheme of all. The Greeks must leave the beach, every tent, every sword, every baloney sandwich packed and stowed away in the ships and the ships must be put to sea. The Trojans would wake up and see the shore deserted and their enemies gone. Gone but for one token: a giant wooden horse constructed of timbers salvaged from some scuttled ships, a monument constructed to commemorate, to memorialize the tumultuous events that transpired upon this beach. But within the horse would be contained a secret. Agamemnon liked the plan, always one to appreciate some deviousness, and he agreed to follow it to the letter.

The Trojan heads popped above the wall to look in and wonder at something none of them had seen in ten years—an empty beach. Before anyone could grab a towel or a beach ball, they saw it—the great wooden horse. They ran to the beach in wonder at the strange sculpture.

DO NOT LITTER BEACH

What was it? What did it mean? A Greek named Sinon, performing as a double agent, answered all questions. The large wooden equine was intended as an offering to the goddess Athena, but those shifty Greeks left it on the beach without an explanation knowing that the Trojans would come out and destroy it and thus incur the wrath of the deity. A parting shot from the losing team so to speak. Can't fool us, the Trojans cried, we'll just pull it right into the city on these surprisingly convenient wheels and make it the centerpiece of the party. No, one lone citizen of Troy named Laocoon cried, it's a trick! One other citizen had also warned of these "Greeks bearing gifts," but that was Cassandra, daughter of King Priam, and although she was a prophetess extraordinaire, she was cursed with being always ignored. Laocoon was met with a harsher response—Poseidon sent two huge serpents out of the waves and onto the shore to squeeze the juice out of Laocoon and his two sons. After that the Trojans fatefully coined the term "never look a gift horse in the mouth" and dragged the big beastie into the city. The celebration commenced, probably less a drunken revel and more a dignified toast, after all Troy had been besieged for a decade and no one in the city was left unscathed.

Eventually, the weary Trojans turned to their beds to rest in what they thought would be peace, but as candles and lamps were blown out the horse gave birth to a squad of very stiff Greek soldiers with the mastermind Odysseus among them. They quickly opened the gates to allow the rest of the Greek army, who had spent the day just offshore in their ships, into the walls. Murder, rape, and pillage ensued and the city burned to the ground. King Priam himself was slain by a son of Achilles and he was only the beginning of the list of the dead. Few among the defeated city escaped. The warrior Aeneas and his father and son were some of these lucky few and he would have his own tale to tell, the *Aeneid,* and his own city, Rome, to found. Some others, primarily women, became captives and slaves to the conquerors, rarely a happy outcome. Helen, her lover Paris having been killed in one of the last battles, was returned to her husband Menelaus. The city turned into a funeral pyre, thousands slain, ten years squandered; it seemed a lot to ask just to have one couple renew their wedding vows.

THE ODYSSEY. The Greeks took to their ships yet again and this time they really set sea for all the various islands and city-states of their Greek homeland. Most made it back to their families with little more fuss than the occasional bout of seasickness. One famously had a monumentally difficult time reaching his beloved homeland and his beloved beloveds: That one was Odysseus, the clever fellow whose bright idea had brought the war to a satisfying conclusion for the Greeks. Poor Odysseus, who had in the beginning done his best to sit out the war, was the last of the warriors to return to the friendly shores of home. The first book of the *Odyssey* begins long after Odysseus's travails had begun, but we will push that aside and look at his story chronologically with the occasional glimpse at his beloved isle of Ithaca and the events that transpired in his absence to his dear wife Penelope and son Telemachus. The Greeks had conquered Troy and were exuberantly letting the Trojans know it. Torches set homes ablaze, swords struck heads from fleeing bodies, and terrible crimes were committed in the spirit of victory. Cassandra the prophetess and daughter of Priam (she was the one nobody ever listened to because she had not returned Apollo's amorous advances after he had gifted her with foresight) ran to the Temple of Athena to beg sanctuary of the goddess who had long been the invaders' staunchest ally. No sanctuary was granted by her enemies for they ripped her from the temple and violated all codes of decency. Athena was angry—nobody, not even her beloved Greeks, were allowed such license. The goddess, as the weary victors set sail for home, enlisted Poseidon's aid and he blew up a storm that lasted nine days. Ships were scattered and sunk and the mighty conquerors were lucky if they ever saw the shores of home again. Most of those that still breathed air would, but many found that salt water now filled their lungs.

Odysseus and his ships were carried far from home and at last anchored on the shores of a land of both invitation and terrible danger. This calm island was inhabited by a congenial and handsome race, a race ready to share their easy bounty. They sustained life by eating a flower, the lotus, and they happily offered this enchanted food to their guests. Many of the sailors fell to feasting and as quickly as the lotuses blossomed on their tongues they forgot—the war, their hardships, and all memories of family and home. They were lost forever to the land of the lotus-eaters, but for Odysseus using every ounce of strength to

drag them back to the ships and chain them to the oars. Once safely back at sea they finally remembered what they were about but panged for more, just one taste more of the addictive flower. Days of sailing without sight of land used all the ships' stores and necessitated a stop for more. A fair island presented itself and the seamen gladly stretched their sea legs on dry land once more. This island promised so more than just a place to walk without rocking back and forth. With a little venturing came a great discovery—the island burst with bounty, a huge cave was filled with cheeses, fruits, and a veritable cornucopia of agricultural marvels. As the sailors re-inflated their deflated bellies, they were forced to scramble for hiding places as the cave's inhabitant arrived with his flock of sheep. The troglodyte was a Cyclops, a son of Poseidon of giant size possessed of only one eye that resided smack in the middle of his forehead. The Cyclops laid down a burden of logs and rolled a huge stone in front of the entrance. It didn't take long for the monstrous man to have his "goldilocks moment," for the starving sailors not content with just cheese and grapes had actually taken the liberty of roasting one of his ewes. Odysseus, fast on his feet, explained to Polyphemus, the Cyclops's given name, that they were wandering sailors and thus under Zeus's protection. Polyphemus promptly and inhospitably responded by grabbing two of the crew, bashing their heads against the stone wall, and eating them both to the last bloody crumb. His dinner finished, Polyphemus promptly got a little shut-eye.

Scheming Odysseus concluded that they could not kill the giant in his sleep because they could never remove the stone. No, subtler methods would need to be used. Polyphemus slept through the night and polished off two more sailors for breakfast, and then he was back to the pastures with his sheep—carefully placing the stone back in place. Odysseus set to work having his men sharpen and harden one of the branches the Cyclops had left for his fire. When Polyphemus came home again from a hard day at work, supper was waiting in the form of two more of the hapless Greeks. As the monster belched and picked man-meat out of his teeth, Odysseus presented himself with a sublime dessert. One of the crew had brought a large skin of undiluted wine and this their captain presented to the Cyclops. Lip-smacking enjoyment and giddiness commenced. "What is your name?" Polyphemus inquired of Odysseus.

"I   am

Noman," declared the gracious captive.

"You are so nice, Noman. I'll save you for last." With that Polyphemus entered the gates of slumberland. While snores echoed around the cave Odysseus and his remaining crew took up the pointed log and plunged it into the Cyclops's closed eye. The searing pain awakened Polyphemus. He bellowed. He retched. He cried. The other Cyclops residing in the caves nearby rushed to the abode of their newly blinded cohort. "What is wrong?"

"I have been hurt, my eye destroyed."

"Who did it to you?"

"Noman!"

"No man? Then it must be the gods. You're on your own, big boy."

In the morning, the Cyclops rolled the stone away and the Greeks, clinging tightly to the underside of the sheep's fleece where Polyphemus's hands could not find them, escaped the cave and made all haste to the ships. Odysseus could not resist a little prideful boasting and shouted his true name and particulars to the stumbling Polyphemus, who as it turned out was a pretty good pitcher of stones once he had the direction. The ships sailed off buffeted by stone-cast waves and the promise that Polyphemus's daddy would never let them get away with disfiguring his son. Odysseus had won a battle but his war with the sea was only beginning. After mourning their digested comrades and a few days of fair sailing the wanderers made landfall at the floating island of Aeolus, the god of the winds. Aeolus was in an exceedingly generous mood and bagged all the winds except the west, which would gently blow the sailors home to Ithaca. He gave the bag to Odysseus for safekeeping and with instructions to not open until safely at home.

But Pandora was not the only human whose curiosity had them stoop to opening mysterious parcels they had been told to leave alone. The sailors, within sight of home, opened the bag. The happy tumult of the released winds blew the ships all the way back to Aeolus's island. Aeolus was a sharp breeze to Odysseus's entreaties. No more help would be forthcoming and the wily Greek might as well stop asking for aid from the other gods, as well. Odysseus was scorned and forgotten by Olympus, only to be remembered by those deities that held him in contempt. As the ships neared the island of the Laestrygonians, Odysseus had a terrible premonition— things that were definitely bad were about to become worse. But too late to communicate his feeling to the other eleven ships of the fleet, they entered the harbor. A hellish rain of stones pelted down from the overhanging cliffs. The ships were smashed to splinters, the sailors speared like fish as they floundered in the churning waters. The Laestrygonians, like the Cyclops, had a taste for human flesh, one they indulged for days after this fateful catch.

Odysseus in his one remaining vessel sailed on. The wooded, rocky island of Aeaea was the saddened travelers' next port of call. Odysseus climbed the heights to have a look-see at the landscape, and to make sure no Laestrygonians or their ilk were lurking about. In the distance he spied a clearing in the thick forest cover and what appeared to be some type of structure. A scouting party was selected and off they pushed through the jungle. When they arrived at the beautiful palace, the Greeks were shocked to see the incredible range of fauna that seemed to cohabit the precinct peacefully. Lions, tigers, and bears (oh my), and lambs, pigs, and goats, as well. This was long before the paintings of Edward Hicks's *The Peaceable Kingdom* existed on Aeaea.

But this kingdom was presided over by the dark and beautiful Circe, who greeted them and lulled them into the palace with a song. Circe was a daughter of Helios and, it must be added, a witch. All the besotted mariners, but one, Eurylochus, followed Circe like puppies and couldn't wait to partake of the delicious foods and wines that were presented to them. As they gobbled they metamorphosed into a herd of swine. Eurylochus hightailed it back to the waiting and anxious Odysseus. Not heeding the pleas of his crew, Odysseus belted his sword and headed for the palace to retrieve and hopefully reacquaint his transformed crew to human life. Along the way Hermes stopped him with a warning (luckily not all the gods had deserted Odysseus) not to eat or drink in Circe's palace unless he first ingested a particular herb, which the god just seemed to have in his possession. The sailor ate and thanked Hermes.

Odysseus reached the marble mansion with its varied and friendly pets in no time and was wining and dining with Circe in a wink after that. The witch was shocked to see that man remained man and did not turn into beast. She acknowledged that Odysseus had bested her in this contest and at his insistence undid her earlier magic. Captain and crew were reunited and in such sumptuous environs. Why not gather the entire ship's complement and everyone could enjoy a little rest and relaxation? Indeed—and a year flew by in luxuriating ease. A year spent with moss growing over the memories of home, cobwebs draping the waiting arms of loved ones left behind. Much was happening on Ithaca during that year. Since Odysseus had departed for Troy many years had passed; the decade of the war itself was being added to year by year in his unsuccessful attempts to return. The kingdom was without a king and by good report all the returning heroes of Greece had arrived at their destinations long before it looked as if Ithaca would remain kingless. That is unless Penelope gave up her fruitless pining and took another as husband. Suitors of every stripe and caliber had arrived and, not unlike Circe's visitors, had behaved like pigs at the trough. Choose one of us they cried, and cried, and cried, and their din destroyed any semblance of watchful patience in the small palace.

Penelope consented to do as they asked but only after she finished a weaving she was working on—a final act to honor her dead husband, but in truth it was a bit of cunning that would marvel even her husband, Penelope wove by day and picked apart the weaving at night, thus delaying the finishing of the cloth. Penelope was in love and loyal to Odysseus still and was sure that one day her transient husband would once more grace the island. She was not alone in this believe for Telemachus the baby almost planted on the beach so long ago also felt the bonds of his departed were still binding and ready to weave even tighter the glamour of that longed-for father. So while Telemachus bound and Penelope wove, Odysseus lounged and caroused in the bed of Circe. It was the crewmen that finally prevailed upon Odysseus to once again board the ship and sail for home, but which way to sail, where to go? Although sad to see her paramour depart, Circe had made him a promise long before to help him find his way home if that was ever his desire, and now she had to follow through. First the sailors would undertake a perhaps even more arduous journey—they must sail to the underworld and there seek out Tiresias the blind prophet for information. As an enticement to get Tiresias to speak Circe provided the mariners with a young ram and a black ewe; she didn't, however, provide them with the true identities of the sacrificial animals. Off to hell Odysseus and his bold and homesick adventurers sailed, all the way to the edge of the world. At the edge was a beach and at the end of the beach was a cave. They entered the cave and slaughtered the beasts, carefully draining the blood into a pit and then they stood back to watch the ghosts arrive. The sailors forced them all back until the shade of Tiresias appeared for a little tonic pick-me-up.

Tiresias was a veritable fount of information. He informed Odysseus that he would make it home safely if he made some appeasement to the gods, especially Poseidon, who remained terribly unhappy with him. They must also be very wary on the island of Thrinacia, but barring any other offenses Odysseus would make it home to dispatch the troubles in his own house and to put his feet up and live to a ripe old age. Happy news, indeed. Tiresias floated off to be replaced by the hero's mother who told him specifically about what was going on in Ithaca and that she herself pined to death for her lost son. After her the parade of dead souls grew and the spectacle grew more depressing—Achilles, Agamemnon, Ajax, and on and on the ghosts marched up to sip a little blood and recount their sad stories. Soon the nameless dead had crowded ever closer and the chill wind of fate blew on Odysseus's neck; he beat a hasty retreat all the way back to Circe's island.

Circe had grown accustomed to Odysseus's face and hated to see him go, but provisioned and anxious, the ship's crew set sail again for home. They passed the island of the sirens, sweetly singing their death songs, and skirted it without a hitch—all the crew had stuffed their ears with wax while Odysseus, not about to miss some good tunes, had himself strapped to the mast. The next obstacle to beset the cruise was the fearsome duo of Scylla and Charybdis, "the devil and the deep blue sea." They managed to slip through the monster and the whirlpool but sadly lost six more men. Then they arrived at the isle of Thrinacia that Tiresias had warned them about. They should have just sailed on by but they were tired and sunk even further into gloom with their losses, so they decided to camp for a night on dry land. But, no one was to disturb anything on the island, not the least little berry, under Odysseus's strict orders. Men will be men and when Odysseus awoke it was to the smell of roasting meat. The crew had butchered one of the beautiful oxen they had found roaming about the island and such a fine beast begged to be turned into a fine feast. The cattle belonged to the god Hyperion and needless to say the god was not pleased. For six days, the weather did not permit them to leave, while the sailors enjoyed the steaks and other amenities of the island. When they at last left the shores they were struck with a storm from Zeus's own hand and the ship was broken into matchsticks. Only Odysseus survived clinging to the wreckage. All the other well-fed sailors drowned.

After nine days Odysseus, with all the other flotsam and jetsam, washed up on the beach of the island of Calypso. Calypso may or may not have been a goddess, but she was certainly Odysseus's savior. She nursed the tired and broken man back to a robust good health and then some. She loved him and didn't want to part with his company, so year after year rolled by and as much as our hero appreciated the fond attention, his thoughts wandered closer and closer to his home. He wanted to leave and Calypso was not inclined to let him. Zeus interceded on his behalf and finally Calypso relented. Odysseus built a raft and made like Huck Finn—off to new territories.

Back on Ithaca, things were becoming more strained. The suitors had eventually discovered Penelope's ruse with the weaving—after all it would had to be gigantic for all the work she put into it—and were at the point of forcing her hand in the matter. Telemachus, now a strapping young man, went off on his own voyage to discover the whereabouts of his dear departed pappy. He traveled to the mainland and the various courts of the veterans of the Trojan War but nobody knew his father's whereabouts. At the palace of Menelaus in Sparta, Athena warned the lad to go home as fast as he could, because big doings were about to be done. He sailed home as quickly as a one-masted bireme could get him there. Odysseus had one last port of call before home, one last shipwreck after a storm at sea and the gentle saving grace of another woman, the nymph Leucothea. He was cast on the shores of Scheria naked and salted, not a happy sight for the Princess Nausicaa and her handmaidens. But after their initial shock and Odysseus's winning words they took him in and eventually to the palace of King Alcinous where Odysseus held the rapt attention of the court with his spellbinding tale of high sea adventure and suffering loss. In fact, most of the actual story of his wandering way home in the *Odyssey* was this recounting before King Alcinous and his people.

Finished and exhausted he slept like a baby as a ship was prepared for departure the next morning. Smooth sailing returned him twenty years after he left to the shores of Ithaca. Home again, home again, fiddle-tee-de! The ship of King Alcinous, however, did not fare as well, for upon finding out that it had just transported the despised Odysseus safely home Poseidon turned it to stone and a stone boat does not remain buoyant very long. In this case, it became more of an island and less of a pair of concrete overshoes. King Alcinous, a seafaring man himself, took the bull by the horns and immediately sacrificed him and twelve brothers to the god of the sea and made the waters all smooth again.

HAVE I GOT A STORY TO TELL YOU — BUT FIRST COULD I GET A PAIR OF PANTS?

Odysseus had slept through the entire voyage and awakened alone and confused on Ithaca's shore. Athena stepped in to protect the old fellow and disguised him in the ragged cloak, wrinkled skin, and graying hair of an old beggar to enable him to travel about unperturbed, plot his reemergence to the world of Ithaca, and administer the comeuppance to the leeching suitors that clung to the possibility of Penelope. Odysseus chanced upon the hut the loyal retainer, Eumaeus, and was greeted with kindness and given food and a warm place to sleep. Back from the mainland, Telemachus was led to the hut and Odysseus, out of the sight of his caregiver, revealed himself to his son. There was happiness and joy, but no celebration for there was much to be done.

The returned king instructed his son to remove all the weapons from the great hall of the palace, and after resuming his disguise he made his way to his capitol with Eumaeus. As they stepped their way along to the palace Odysseus's disguise was discovered and his identity happily revealed to one, his former servant and best friend, his now ancient dog Argus. Argus was taking the sun on top of a dungheap and roused as Odysseus came near. He recognized his beloved master and in one final heroic gesture wagged his tail and died. No one else had guessed, but unencumbered with preconceptions the dog had seen directly into the heart of truth and love. Odysseus certainly paused in his march to stroke the old dog's head and Homer reported that he "wiped a salty tear."

They continued. Within the hall the suitors' bullying ways were in full swing and it was no time before the old beggar was mistreated by the parasitic braggarts. Penelope in true queenly fashion came to Odysseus's aid, and although there was no recognition, there was a connection. Odysseus suggested that she pit the suitors in one last contest to string the great bow of Odysseus and then to fire an arrow through the gaps left between twelve axes driven into the wall. Penelope was most agreeable to this plan and wasted nary a syllable in announcing this final challenge to the suitors. Only a man the equal of Odysseus's strength and skill would be worthy for her to take as husband to her bed. The wanderer had, however, had been recognized by one other of the court. In an act of loving kindness, Penelope had bid one her maidservants to wash the old beggar's feet, and this woman identified Odysseus by a scar on his leg. Eurycleia had been his nursemaid many years before and she knew the old injury like a mother knows the last little freckle on her baby's bald head. Odysseus bid her keep silent and added her to the growing confederacy.

The queen insisted that the contest begin. Nobody was happy to compete and nobody was able to string the great bow when they were given the opportunity. Then the old beggar asked to be given a chance and to the amazement of all promptly fitted the string over the bow's end. Telemachus escorted his amazed mother out of the chamber, Eurycleia barred one door, another loyal servant, Philoetius, barred another at Eumaeus's command, and Odysseus, with the ease of a horse flicking a fly off his backside, nocked his arrow to the string and released. The arrow flew straight as a swallow through the axes. And then with a reveal that left the suitors in a state of shock, Odysseus threw his beggar's rags to the side and the carnage began. Telemachus, Eumaeus, and Philoetius joined Odysseus with spears in hand. The suitors managed to arm themselves after they found an unlocked way into the armory. Arrows, swords, and spears flew in the enclosed space. Blood splashed against the walls like they were being given a sloppy paint job. Brains and bone splattered and clattered across the flagstones. Four against the tens of men anxious to take Odysseus's wife and his kingdom proved that a few could hold the day in a righteous cause. Like the refuse of a tornado, bodies littered the great hall in a twisted grotesque heap and Odysseus and his son and two loyals stood above the fray. Only two suitors were spared, a bard and a herald, decent fellows who had never exploited their situation and who just might tell Odysseus's tale—a hero never shies away from a little publicity.

Back and in charge, Odysseus ordered the servant girls, who had been the playthings of the suitors and had participated in the abuse of his home and its inhabitants, to clean the horrific mess before they were taken out and hanged for their troubles. Others who had been disloyal, abusive, or opportunistic in his absence were executed in sometimes barbaric and terrible fashion. But all was not right yet in the kingdom. The men that had met their untimely ends were from the prominent families, and on receipt of the news, they stormed to the palace for revenge. Leartes, Odysseus's old dad, was furious at the treatment and disloyalty displayed by the people of the kingdom and proved that Odysseus was indeed just a chip off the old block by hurling a spear with deadly accuracy into the breast of the lead insurrectionist.

Zeus gave Athena a powerful nudge to bring some peace into the proceedings and some semblance of order was restored. Only one holdout remained, Penelope, she who had waited for what seemed like an eternity for this day, was still wary of this man, this stranger. Was he or wasn't he? She ordered the marriage bed to be placed outside their sleeping chamber for him to occupy until she was assured of his identity. Odysseus argued it was impossible because the main bedpost was actually a living tree that grew from floor to ceiling in the room. It was Odysseus!

HONEY, I'M HOME.

Happiness was restored. Joy abounded. The cursed wanderer had returned home. Homer doesn't tell us how Odysseus lived the rest of his life or how he died. He did have Tiresias say that if Odysseus placated the gods with a libation or two he would live to a ripe old age. Another epic, the *Telegonia,* that deals with our adventurer and his travails says that there had been a prophecy that Odysseus would die at the hands of his son, not faithful Telemachus, but a son he had by Circe. Dante has Odysseus sailing off into the Atlantic and pumping into the mount of purgatory and ending up in hell as an ever-burning flame. Even the modern Greek writer, Nikos Kazantzakis, got into the melee with his *Odyssey: A Modern Sequel* in which our hero gets bored with domesticity and sails off again to more adventures and a finale in Antarctica. All good stories, but I like Homer's, to think of the aging Odysseus sitting at home with a grandchild or two on his knees telling them the story of the Cyclops, or the music of the Sirens, or just nodding off to indulge in a discrete little appreciation of Circe or Calypso. Then maybe one day while he dozes in the sun before his hall he awakes to find old Argus, but young again, come to fetch him for a hunt or a romp, and maybe just over the hill waiting on the beach are his crew and a well-provisioned ship. And thus Odysseus ends his adventures—at least, it's what I'd like to think.

PART III.

A FUNNY THING HAPPENED ON THE WAY FROM ANCIENT GREECE TO THE MODERN WORLD —WE REMEMBERED

The temples have fallen. The scrolls have crumbled into dust. The world of Heracles and Homer is long gone and so much has happened in between. And yet we remember these stories. They still have meaning and stir our emotions. Why do we care? In some sense they are not just rousing tales of action and adventure, tragedy and grief; they are a catalogue of our internal and eternal emotions and desires. But before we get too Freudian about it, let's take a little jaunt with these myths through the history that carried them down to us. Even as the great civilization of Greece was becoming long in the tooth and bent with age, a new champion was being born—one who would spread the stories further than ever before and take them under new and mutating influences. In some ways this golden-locked young hero joined the Olympians in the pantheon, and assuredly nudged a few to the side in the process. This hardy boy was none other than Alexander the Great. Alexander was a Macedonian, not actually a Greek, and a bit of a convert to all things Greco. His teachers were Greek, Aristotle chief among them, and his sensibilities were fashioned in the classical mode. When he conquered Greece, he made sure to export his version of it along with his Greek troops to all the corners of the mysterious flat earth in which he battled. From India to Egypt his sword and his mania transformed the world. Zeus conjoined Brahma, Thebes became an Egyptian city, and the Sphinx flew back to the motherland. The world became a little bit more global and a little bit more Greek, but nothing could equal the conversion of the next great Mediterranean civilization and its lasting influence.

1. ROME

The all-conquering, all-consuming, capitol city of the Italian peninsula, Rome, regurgitated the Greek myths over the world— and crucifixion awaited if you didn't like it. The Romans in many ways considered Greek civilization effeminate and soft compared to their virile machine of law and conquest, but for all of that, they sure liked those myths. They took their own gods and transposed them over the old Greeks: Zeus became Jupiter, Hera became Juno, Poseidon became Neptune, Hades became Pluto, Hermes became Mercury, Hestia became Vesta, Ares became Mars, Athena became Minerva, Aphrodite became Venus, Artemis became Diana, Hephaestus became Vulcan, Dionysus became Bacchus, and Apollo, being Apollo, got to remain Apollo. The transposition affected many of the heroes; Hercules became Heracles, Persephone became Proserpina, and so on.

Many of the myths come down to us from their Roman sources, like Ovid's *Metamorphoses*, while the original Greek tellings are lost in time. The Romans also got into the business of copying Greek statuary, so many of the images familiar to us of the gods and goddesses are actually copies of the earlier originals. Greek architecture also fell into the great Roman digesting engine and until the advent of the arch and the dome, Latin temples followed the basic post (Ionic,

172

Dorian, and Corinthian columns) and lintel (just like those bas-relief friezes that decorated the pediments they knew so well) system of their forbears to the East.

When the poet Vergil sat down with pen at the scroll, the Romans even formulated a wonderful myth of the creation of their city, the *Aeneid,* that firmly established their classical bona fides. Aeneas, the Trojan son of Venus, escaped the destruction of Troy with his father on his back and with his son by the hand. Like that old Ithacan, he wandered about the world of the Mediterranean with his loyal refugees encountering bleeding plants, harpies, Scylla and Charybdis, various prophets and oracles, and even old blind Polyphemus the Cyclops, eventually landing on the shores of Carthage and enjoying the admiration of the beautiful Queen Dido. But alas, his destiny must be followed to other shores and the founding of a new Troy.

However, the Trojans first stopped in Sicily and were so popular with the women there that the ladies conspired to burn their ships to keep them on the island, but Jupiter sent a rainstorm and the remaining ships were off to the Italian mainland. Before exploring much of this new country Aeneas had another journey in mind—he wanted to visit his father Anchises, who died back in Carthage. With the Sibyl, yet another oracle, in tow and a glowing golden bough in hand, Aeneas traveled to the underworld. And after a little set-to with Cerberus and the always acerbic Chiron, he arrived at Elysium, the new abode of dear old dad. Anchises was overjoyed to see his offspring and in his prophesying spells out the lineage to come from Romulus, a great grandson many times over of Aeneas to come, and the actual founder of Rome, to the Emperor Augustus, who just happened to be the ruler when Vergil was scribbling his epic. In a similar fashion to the *Iliad,* a great deal of turmoil both on earth and in the heavens would ensue before there was any happiness in this new land of Latium.

The whole story ends with a mortal combat between Aeneas, who has become an ally of the Latiums, and a king of the Rutulians named Turnus who doesn't care much for his neighbor's alliance with these interloping Trojans. Of course, various gods provided various weapons to the combatants, and in the end, Aeneas slew Turnus, because he saw he was wearing Athena's sword-belt. The eventual founding of Rome by those Anean descendents and twins Romulus and Remus was assured. In time that city, that empire founded by those twins (maybe their belligerence, and those Romans who followed them, came from the milk they suckled from the she-wolf that raised them) dwindled and crumbled into dust like all those that came before.

A new global enterprise was on the ascent and it had no love for the tales of gods and goddesses. Christianity controlled the world of Europe and the few tales that were remembered were consigned to the bin of superstition and witchcraft. A new dark age had arrived. But what goes around comes back around. Toward the end of this middle age the myths started to resurface, to be refitted and find new ground in the culture. First a certain long-beaked Italian named Dante reclaimed a great treasure trove of gods and monsters and retold their stories in his great poem, *The Divine Comedy.* Most of these figures of wonder, from Odysseus to Geryon to Midas and the Harpies, found themselves consigned to the rings of hell, but you have to start somewhere and thus they were remembered. After Dante, other writers and artists started to play with some of those exciting tales of yesteryear. Scholars rediscovered the forgotten manuscripts and workmen with shovels and picks accidentally unearthed a past that most had forgotten. A renewed interest in the imaginary world of ancient Greece was blossoming. One might even call it a "rebirth."

2. THE RENAISSANCE

Rebirth, renaissance—a renewed excitement in all things ancient; a harkening back to those earlier times when things were "pure" and unclouded with the uncertainties of 15th-century Italy. As statuary was unearthed and cleaned to the stark and resplendent white of marble, or even the dense greens of tarnished bronze, a new and inaccurate view of the old civilization of Greece was being formed. What has been passed down to us is only now a little closer to the truth, as we have discovered that Greek sculptures and the temples that housed them were brightly painted, a veritable Dionysian frenzy of bright colors. Greece was a world of glory, of beauty, of clear-eyed democrats that viewed their place in the universe through their multiplicity of gods with a profound sense of connection and a devotion to the simpler Edenic world.

I LOVE MY GOD, BUT, MAN, I LIKE THESE STORIES!

DIVINE COMEDY

We can still see the Renaissance misinterpretation in the grand and lovely paintings of Botticelli. To gaze at his *Birth of Venus* in the Uffizi in Florence is like seeing, feeling the budding and opening of blooms in springtime, but not just experiencing the transformation of Winter as an outside observer—it is like being one with the bud. You sense the pleasant breeze from Zephyr raising the hairs on your arms, you smell the blossoms that Flora strew about her, and you ache to worship at the shell-supported feet of the goddess of love in all her naked beauty. Botticelli repeated his praise in many paintings and it was praise to the mistaken understanding of our ancient myths. But who can complain at such misunderstanding when so much wondrous glory is created anew?

I BETTER THROW A BLANKET OVER THIS WHOLE BUSINESS.

Botticelli was only one of the company of artists presenting this grander world of myth to an admiring public—until the inevitable backlash to such pagan displays under the tutelage of men like the monk Savonarola whipped their cohorts into "bonfires of the vanities," which turned lovely creations into ashes. Even Botticelli participated in the destruction of some of his works. Art won out in the wars of history and we can still stand in awe before the paintings of Raphael, Giorgione, Caravaggio, and Titian and the sculptures of Michelangelo, Cellini, and Bernini (take a look at Bernini's *Daphne and Apollo* to be stirred at the nymph's moment of metamorphosis into the laurel tree).

This reconstruction of the ancient world also informed art that was totally in the realm of the sacred, and by sacred we mean Christian. A new sensibility and sensuality flows through even the most reverent Madonna and even the maddest of saints. It took a while, but this warmth eventually flowed northward and informed those artists in frostier climes. In the world of literature and scholarship the great epics and treatises were having the dust blown off them and once more were unrolled before eager eyes. Alchemy with all its allusions to classical mythology was flourishing and one could not be considered truly sophisticated and urbane without having some working knowledge of our legendary past. There was no doubt that at last the myths were here to stay, even when they might have undergone their own metamorphosis in the process.

3. NEO-CLASSICISM

The Renaissance, much like the myths they had rediscovered, was a time of excitement and profound and ingenerating chaos. Knowledge gave forth to rebellion and invention. Guttenberg's printing press allowed this knowledge and opinion to be spread throughout Europe. The monolithic church was shattered into pieces—retaining a foothold in some states but being swept away and replaced in others. Science was forcing its way to prevalence in the world of human thought while witch hunters and inquisitions kept the light of ignorance burning bright. But the lights of reformation and revolution were blinding the horrific glow of human shish-ka-bobs and torches soaked in fear. And that light became known as the Enlightenment.

The Enlightenment was powered by reason, by the quest for understanding not just in the old superstitious ways of intuiting by emotion but by sound logical problem solving. The efforts of Socrates, Plato, and Aristotle, though sometimes woefully incorrect in their assumptions, strove to find supporting evidence to bolster or dash a claim; they often erred because they lived in a time and place where that information was denied to them. This new enlightened age is the age of Isaac Newton and his mathematical theories, of gravity and thermodynamics, of the wit and authority-snubbing wisdom of Voltaire, of revolutionary thinkers like Thomas Jefferson and the radical Thomas Paine.

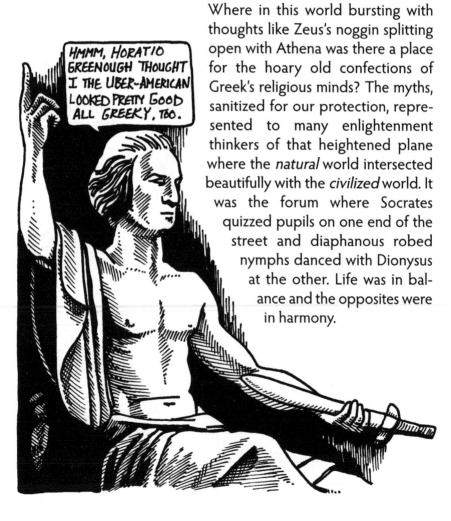

Where in this world bursting with thoughts like Zeus's noggin splitting open with Athena was there a place for the hoary old confections of Greek's religious minds? The myths, sanitized for our protection, represented to many enlightenment thinkers of that heightened plane where the *natural* world intersected beautifully with the *civilized* world. It was the forum where Socrates quizzed pupils on one end of the street and diaphanous robed nymphs danced with Dionysus at the other. Life was in balance and the opposites were in harmony.

These sentiments built on some Renaissance presumptions about classical art—clear, untainted, and unsullied with riots of color—and continued through the Mannerists into the Baroque and into Neo-Classicism. The Baroque had been a playground of the gods, the fields of the Elysium, where wine flowed and gods, putti, and satyrs laughed. The Neo-Classicists shunned much of the frivolity; after all it smacked of the excesses of the kings the Enlightenment had turned against. They celebrated the clean lines, the purity of form, and the rational gaze of the classics they admired. These new gods were painted and sculpted with the clarity of Jacques Louis David, where even the death of the bloody revolutionary Marat is given an Olympian grandeur, sculpted with the elegance of Jean Antoine Houdon, and even reflected in the noble architecture of buildings public and private from the Pantheon in Paris to Thomas Jefferson's home in Monticello. The

United States' own first democratically elected head of state, George Washington, assumes the pose of a modern Zeus in the commemorative sculpture of Horatio Greenough erected in the Smithsonian Institution. Fashion followed suit with Empire gowns based on a reworking of ancient costuming, down to the Phrygian cap of the French *sans culottes* (revolutionaries), the same cap old Midas used to cover his ass ears.

But times change and the starkness of Neo-Classicism was pushed aside by the emotionalism of Romanticism—the passion for Greece displayed by the brushwork of Eugene Delacroix and the poetry of Lord Byron (who cared so much about Greece he died in its revolution). Eventually the massive kitsch attack of the French Salon and the English Victorian painters almost buried the myths and the mythologized history of Greece in layers of lovingly rendered but terribly overwrought paint. The gooey sentimentality embedded in the canvases of William-Adolphe Bouguereau and the melodrama of Sir Lawrence Alma-Tadema could almost coat the myths in an impenetrable layer and obscure them forever, but other minds were at work in other fields and the myths emerged once again with startling, if not always accurate, clarity. Deep into the psyche we must travel.

4. NIETZSCHE

If a moustache would ever qualify one for entrance to Mount Olympus Nietzsche would be first in line. This German philosopher with the broom sprouting from beneath his nose revived a certain serious interest in the old gods of Greece and posited the possibility of each individual to become one. He also famously declared that god was dead. In the labyrinth of his fertile mind he saw all kinds of possibilities, and plenty of impossibilities, too. Friedrich Nietzsche was born a child of extreme German nationalism and terrible German frustration. The Kaiser wanted to unify all those territories he considered part of the German homeland but was constantly being thwarted in his desires by obstacles like France.

This is the pot that young Freddy's sensibilities were boiled in and it informs his first book *The Birth of Tragedy.* At the root of this study of Greece's great dramatic invention is a dilemma: If the god Dionysus is the god of wine and wild debauch how can tragedy be a celebration devoted to him? And why did Tragedy as this supreme art form fade so quickly? Nietzsche waded through some philosophical Aegean stables, much of which deals with the ultra-rational and often depressed chorus of the tragedy. The chorus functions as that voice, some might call the "nay-saying mother" that resides somewhere to the rear of your head telling you "no, you shouldn't" and "life is doomed and then you die." It's grim stuff, but the chorus doesn't just say it: they dance it and sing it and it becomes transformed into enjoyment for the audience. That transformation is the Dionysian moment. The moment to go wild—to say to heck with it all, let's party! Or maybe not. Nietzsche posited that tragedy eventually faded, because the delivery style of the chorus changed—no more song and dance, just the spoken unhappy word.

From chitons and sandals Nietzsche moved to horned helms and magic swords. Freddy discovered Richard Wagner. But old Wagner still had a bit of the Greek in him buried somewhere in his uber-Germanic cells, because he called his music "Dionysian" and his drama "Apollonian." Within in those notes and arias a different mythology was explored the cold, harsh world of the Teutonic gods. Sure, it involved the same incestuous relations, the same family bickering, the same treachery, and occasional fits of nobility, but it is never a romp in the glades of Arcadia. The Greeks gave us grapes and the Teutons give us turnips.

Eventually, even Wagner wasn't quite big enough for Nietzsche's boots; an even bigger size was needed and, like some displaced

Bellerophon, he pulled on his size 12s and stomped to Olympus. Once there he threw the gods over the balustrades and took up residence himself. Man becomes *Uber-mensche*, the "Over-man." This exalted position wasn't just for everyone, only the select few with the strength and intelligence to force themselves out of the common herd and the will to takeover their own destiny. Nietzsche saw Christianity and most of Western thought leading to *nihilism*, nothingness, and it would take these superior beings out of the darkness and into the light. But, alas, try as he might Nietzsche wasn't quite that man. After witnessing a man savagely beating a horse, the philosopher was admitted to a psychiatric hospital in Basel, Switzerland, in 1889. He spent the next decade being nursed by his mother away from the world and died in 1900. His sister set about publishing all his work and flirting with a leader who would pervert her brother's ideas and try to literally build a world of real monstrous "over-men." This was a fellow with a pinched little moustache (not the generous passionate growth of Nietzsche), a fellow named Adolph Hitler.

5. FREUD

Sixteen years after Nietzsche was born another German-speaking visitor to the land of myth was born. In every way his was the more important visit, because he still has more relevance, even in disrepute, than old Friedrich would ever have. This Jewish lad, raised by a stern father and an attractive mother, developed all sorts of conditions and complexes as a child that would serve him well later in life. If you have never heard of Sigmund Freud and his reinterpretation of Greek mythology, then you have not only failed to pay attention in class, but you have also failed to pay attention in life. Sigmund Freud is the father of psychoanalysis. Before his work in the field some great minds prevailed, but no one had ever taken it to the heights and depths that he did. Freud went far beyond "hysteria," the condition that many frustrated women found themselves diagnosed with. Throwing one blanket over the great suffering lot, he was able to discern many disorders with his "talking cure."

But it is Freud's study of men and himself in particular that gave rise to the greatest mythological conceit of the modern world: the Oedipus complex. On a train trip Freud accidentally spied his mother naked. In his preadolescent way he desired her. He was also terribly afraid of his father, a demanding and belittling man who seemed to have nothing but criticism for his young son. These basics percolated in Freud's cranium through dreams and waking hours and eventually came to a brew when overplayed with the myth of Oedipus. Yes, Freud wanted to kill his "castrating" papa just the way Oedipus had done his old man in at that fateful crossroads, and he wanted to marry, or at least bed, his mama just the way

Oedipus had done his mom, Jocasta. This was a eureka moment for Freud, not just because it helped him explain himself to himself, but also because he could apply it in various ways to so many of the male patients he was seeing. He was also overjoyed to "discover" that dreams weren't just a surrealistic jumble of fright and nonsense, but they revealed the path to truly discerning one's most potent desires.

Sigmund was off like a greyhound after a rabbit. For from oral to anal to genital and through latency to full-blown adult neurosis, sex was what drove us. Like Zeus and every woman not his wife Hera we were the puppets of our sexual desires. Poor old Oedipus hadn't just stumbled into Thebes and accidentally fallen into bed with his mother—that is where he most desired to be. Women were often afflicted with a parallel condition known as the Electra complex, named after Agamemnon's daughter who had an affection for her dear departed dad that stood in the way of her getting on in life.

JA, I MUSTA BEEN A BEAUTIFUL BABY...

Another of Freud's great contributions to our world of thought and an apt reference to our Greek forbears was his the condition of narcissism. Like Narcissus, that beautiful boy that Aphrodite had cursed to fall in love with his own reflection, those cursed with narcissism were doomed to hold only themselves in regard. It was an auto-erotic desire that precluded true desire for another. This condition is often seen as the true condition of the modern and postmodern condition. We are a world of naval gazers and our mapmaker into this world of solipsistic reflection is none other than its definer.

But these complexes weren't the end of it for Freud; he used myth in many ways. The allusions to the gods and goddesses, heroes, and monsters were myriad and constituted an entire Trojan horse–load of penises and vaginas just waiting to see the light of day. Freud died in 1939 but there are few alive that don't still see his reflection gazing over our shoulder when we look into the mirror.

6. POPULAR CULTURE

Like Odysseus our voyage has been long but at last we have landed on the shores of our own contemporary Ithaca, and boy has our home changed. We are a post-Freudian, post-postmodern, narcissistic and plugged-in collection of complexes and neuroses in need of instant gratification. Those myths just keep coming back to haunt us.

BOOKS. Probably a whole forest of trees has gone into retellings of the Greek myths. Chief among these reinterpreters is Thomas Bulfinch. He dared go where many had gone before but he did it with a Victorian can-do attitude that would enlighten decades to come. *The Age of Fable,* along with *The Age of Chivalry* and *Legends of Charlemagne*, still serves as the cornerstone to many a mythological collection. Edith Hamilton's *Mythology* would closely follow old Bulfinch on any bookshelf. *Mythology* is a glorious and easily understood compendium of all the myths that are "fit to print," with even a few of the Norse myths thrown in for good measure. *The Larousse Encyclopedia of Mythology* was an attempt to cover just about every mythological cycle, not just our beloved Greeks, in as concise a fashion as possible. Different editions of the *Encyclopedia* have taken that concision to lesser or greater lengths, sometimes in multiple volumes.

These pathfinders have led in their different ways to the entire cottage industry of retellers. Some, like Robert Graves (his book *The White Goddess* posits a veritable war among the sexes with the matriarchy being overthrown by the patriarchy in both heaven and on earth), have created an entirely new framework to see the myths through, and many have simply enjoyed spinning these Penelope threads to visualize their own singular, if not revolutionary, vision of the old well-worn tales.

In the world of fiction the gods have been invented and reinvented as if revisions instead of evils had been released from Pandora's box. The gods have taken the pages in worlds of ancient fantasy and in the grey flannel suits of the modern world. Both stories for children and decidedly adult novels have tried to explain or simply delight in the myths. Pan is an elusive character in tales as different as Kenneth Grahame's wonderful tales of the domestic lives of the forest creatures in *The Wind in the Willows* to James Stephen's wonderfully askew *The Crock of Gold*. The old goat-footed one can still summon a bit of the old panic in tales like Arthur Machen's *The Great God Pan*. The entire pantheon shows up in Thorne Smith's *Night Life of the Gods*, a book that makes one wonder if William Powell might be Zeus. John Erskine also penned novels about Helen of Troy, Odysseus, and Venus along with a wide array of other subjects pulled from the world of legend and myth. Erskine, although sadly forgotten today,

C'MON TO TOAD HALL AND WE'LL PAR-TAY!

still makes for some good urbane and witty reading. In a more serious vein, Mary Renault built many "historical" novels around mythological themes. The tale of Theseus and his duke-out with the Minotaur is given the full treatment in her novels *The Bull from the Sea* and *The King Must Die*.

In a more literary vein we have the British sculptor Michael Ayrton's superb reworking of the story of the inventor who not only aided in the conception of the Minotaur but designed his elaborate prison; *The Maze Maker* is an understanding treatment of Daedalus by a man who not only was fascinated with his myth but also attempted to reproduce some of his feats. The aforementioned Robert Graves, besides doing his own anthology of the Greek myths, also wrote novels reimagining some of them, like *Hercules, My Shipmate*, a somewhat different account of the cruise of the Argo. Graves also took a trip across the Bosporus to visit the Trojan War in his novels *The Anger of Achilles* and *Homer's Daughter*. Greece's great and petulant hero of that war is also the subject of Madeline Miller's recent *The Song of Achilles* in which she imagines something a little more between the Achilles and Patroclus than cousinly love.

Modern poetry has also looked back to that earlier world with epics like Nikos Kazantzakis's *Odyssey: A Modern Sequel* (and that is just what it is) and Christopher Logue's powerful poems based on the *Iliad*, *War Music*, and *Kings*. These and their cohorts are often worth the trip.

COMICS. In a medium of much fewer words and a lot more pictures, comic books have been kind to the Greek myths and the myths have been super-kind to them. There have certainly been many treatments and retellings in the form of those paneled pages—*Classics Illustrated* had generations of young Americans reading versions of Homer and some of the more palatable stories of younger appetites—but it is tucked within the pages of comics with names like *Action Comics* and *Marvel Tales* that these pencilers have done their utmost to hearken back and to make a mythological world anew. Certainly the actual gods and heroes of the myths have made their appearances within the pages—Hercules has been both enemy and sometimes companion to that god of a rivaling mythology, Thor—but it is in the comics most important and informing form that the myths have been truly made fresh.

The "superhero" is in every way possible a reinvention of the ancients in brightly colored spandex instead of linen and bronze. Superman is certainly a god exiled from his Mount Olympus, Krypton, to fare as best he can among the mere mortals of Smallville and Metropolis. Other heroes like Spiderman are made demigods not by the "accident" of having a divine progenitor but the actions of that modern divinity—science. Sometimes nuclear radiation, mysterious beams from space, a homemade brew of chemicals, whatever the agency—ordinary seekers are turned into mighty beings for good and ill. What is a good comic story without an equally powerful super villain? These new myths always hold out the possibility, no matter how remote, that the reader might one day stumble into a situation, a formula that can transform them into one of these new Olympians.

MOVIES. But even with all the world-circumnavigating and time traveling a good comic can do, it has a hard time competing with the real "being there" that a movie plunges you into. The early days of cinema were perhaps a little afraid to attempt visiting the world of Greek mythology—heck, they were often busy creating their own mythology—but as sophistication with the medium grew so did the attempts to take happy filmgoers by the scruff of the imagination and fly them to those older times. None did this more successfully or inspirationally than the great stop-motion animator, Ray Harryhausen. Harryhausen learned his craft at the knee of Willis O'Brian, the animator of *King Kong,* an apt competitor for the Titans if ever there was one, and who went on to almost single-handedly make of this creaky medium a new and unimagined poetry. His forays into the world of the Aegean and its fabulous tales has given us *Jason and the Argonauts* and *Clash of the Titans,* and these two films along with his other adventure movies opened to the Saturday matinee voyager and sometimes the more sophisticated adult viewer a realm of possibility. *Clash* has recently been remade, losing some of the charm of the original animation to computer graphics, and has not only taken us for gut-swirling 3D gallops aboard Pegasus but has also added a phrase to our popular culture, "Release the Kraken!" (never mind that the kraken is a denizen of an entirely different mythology). *Clash* also led to an almost inevitable sequel, *Wrath of the Ti-*

ME! You WANT RELEASED?

tans, and one can only imagine that the Titans are going to remain blissfully wrathful at the box office for some time to come.

The Trojan War was recreated in the film *Troy* and this time not even Brad Pitt could help the war keep from trapping the viewers in a Trojan horse of boredom, but we still must honor those valiant geeks of filmland for trying. *The Immortals,* directed by Tarsem (director and writer of the incredible film *The Fall* with its references to many mythologies), couldn't stir much excitement even with the freeing of the imprisoned and vengeful Titans. A little more excitement is generated with *300,* based on Frank Miller's graphic novel wherein history is mythologized, homoeroticized, and glamorized; even a god or two appears in the sepia murk somewhere. Firmly in the realm of the kiddies but more fun than some of the fare aimed at an older clientele is *Percy Jackson & the Olympians: The Lightning Thief,* which comes by way of the series of young adult novels by Rick Riordan. Riordan imagines that the gods are still very much alive in our contemporary world and still coupling with mortals to generate new and gifted offspring. *Percy* and company are returning in a sequel that may not be the *Odyssey* but which will certainly be more fun than some of the films with more serious intentions aimed at older customers. Other films with connections to the Greek myths exist in the cinemas and on television waiting for all you demigods to discover. After all, you can't sit back and wait for Prometheus to bring them to you.

THERE'S MORE BEEF CAKE IN 300 THAN IN McDONALDS

CONCLUSION

This has been an attempt to acquaint the reader with the best-known Greek myths. It has not been an exhaustive nor a scholarly study, but is intended more of a romp in the fields of Arcady, a way to become acquainted. And please remember that these stories are ever with us and, in one form or another, will ever be. Some predate our notions of civilization, some sprang full-grown like Athena from the head of Zeus, and some rewrite themselves continuously in our deepest urges. We may not know or understand them, but they are with us and will remain. This brings to mind a tale:

Zeus and Hermes descended the crags of Mount Olympus to observe human beings as they actually are and not as they present themselves to the gods. They wandered the world in disguise, everywhere finding inhospitality, indifference, and sometimes abuse. At last, their steps brought them before the woven-reed door of a poor hovel in the wilds of Phrygia. They called through the door, and an old man, Philemon, and his old wife, Baucis, responded from the darkness within. Without hesitation the couple invited the strangers into their crude dwelling and presented them with the only seats in the house while they proceeded to prepare the finest supper they could for their guests. A little bread, a little honey, and a few drops of wine were all they could readily offer. But the couple could see that this was too small a repast for these noble strangers and Philemon attempted to capture the goose, their companion of many years, for Baucis to throw into the pot. Zeus immediately halted the goose chase and revealed himself in all his glory to the old ones. Hermes followed suit and Philemon and Baucis dropped to their knees before the visiting gods. The gods took them up by the hand and out of the hut. With a sweep of his arm Zeus turned the scrub marsh around into gardens to rival those of the wealthiest palace, and the rough wooden pillars of the hut grew into marble and wattle walls smoothed into granite.

"THIS IS MY TEMPLE AND YOU ARE MY CARETAKERS— FOR AS YOU HAVE TAKEN CARE OF ME WITH KINDNESS, SO SHALL I TAKE CARE OF YOU. DO YOU DESIRE ANYTHING IN ALL OF HEAVEN AND EARTH?"

The kind old couple had only one wish—when the time came for them to part this world for the next, they would leave it together.

So the years went by and Philemon and Baucis cared for the temple of Zeus and continued to offer hospitality to all who came their way, and then the day arrived when they must go. With hands entwined and eyes locked they breathed their last goodbyes of love. Zeus encircled them with bark and leaf and they transformed into an oak and a linden tree both miraculously growing from the selfsame trunk.

The temple has fallen into ruin and gone, but there in the far hills of Phrygia the tree grows still. And like the tree the myths live still, and they send forth seeds to cultivate ever fresh and fertile lands.

JOE LEE is an illustrator, cartoonist, writer, and clown. With a degree from Indiana University centering on Medieval History, Joe is also a graduate of Ringling Brothers, Barnum and Bailey's Clown College. He worked for some years as a circus clown. He is the illustrator of a baker's dozen of For Beginners books, including *Barack Obama*, *Shakespeare*, *Postmodernism*, *Deconstruction*, *Eastern Philosophy*, *Dante*, *Jane Austen* and *Global Warming* among others. Joe lives in Bloomington, Indiana with his wife Mary Bess, son Brandon, cat George, and the terriers (or rather terrors) Max and Jack.

THE FOR BEGINNERS® SERIES

AFRICAN HISTORY FOR BEGINNERS: ISBN 978-1-934389-18-8

ANARCHISM FOR BEGINNERS: ISBN 978-1-934389-32-4

ARABS & ISRAEL FOR BEGINNERS: ISBN 978-1-934389-16-4

ART THEORY FOR BEGINNERS: ISBN 978-1-934389-47-8

ASTRONOMY FOR BEGINNERS: ISBN 978-1-934389-25-6

AYN RAND FOR BEGINNERS: ISBN 978-1-934389-37-9

BARACK OBAMA FOR BEGINNERS, AN ESSENTIAL GUIDE: ISBN 978-1-934389-44-7

BLACK HISTORY FOR BEGINNERS: ISBN 978-1-934389-19-5

THE BLACK HOLOCAUST FOR BEGINNERS: ISBN 978-1-934389-03-4

BLACK WOMEN FOR BEGINNERS: ISBN 978-1-934389-20-1

CHOMSKY FOR BEGINNERS: ISBN 978-1-934389-17-1

DADA & SURREALISM FOR BEGINNERS: ISBN 978-1-934389-00-3

DANTE FOR BEGINNERS: ISBN 978-1-934389-67-6

DECONSTRUCTION FOR BEGINNERS: ISBN 978-1-934389-26-3

DEMOCRACY FOR BEGINNERS: ISBN 978-1-934389-36-2

DERRIDA FOR BEGINNERS: ISBN 978-1-934389-11-9

EASTERN PHILOSOPHY FOR BEGINNERS: ISBN 978-1-934389-07-2

EXISTENTIALISM FOR BEGINNERS: ISBN 978-1-934389-21-8

FDR AND THE NEW DEAL FOR BEGINNERS: ISBN 978-1-934389-50-8

FOUCAULT FOR BEGINNERS: ISBN 978-1-934389-12-6

GENDER & SEXUALITY FOR BEGINNERS: ISBN 978-1-934389-69-0

GLOBAL WARMING FOR BEGINNERS: ISBN 978-1-934389-27-0

HEIDEGGER FOR BEGINNERS: ISBN 978-1-934389-13-3

ISLAM FOR BEGINNERS: ISBN 978-1-934389-01-0

JANE AUSTEN FOR BEGINNERS: ISBN 978-1-934389-61-4

JUNG FOR BEGINNERS: ISBN 978-1-934389-76-8

KIERKEGAARD FOR BEGINNERS: ISBN 978-1-934389-14-0

LACAN FOR BEGINNERS: ISBN 978-1-934389-39-3

LINGUISTICS FOR BEGINNERS: ISBN 978-1-934389-28-7

MALCOLM X FOR BEGINNERS: ISBN 978-1-934389-04-1

MARX'S *DAS KAPITAL* FOR BEGINNERS: ISBN 978-1-934389-59-1

MCLUHAN FOR BEGINNERS: ISBN 978-1-934389-75-1

NIETZSCHE FOR BEGINNERS: ISBN 978-1-934389-05-8

PHILOSOPHY FOR BEGINNERS: ISBN 978-1-934389-02-7

PLATO FOR BEGINNERS: ISBN 978-1-934389-08-9

POETRY FOR BEGINNERS: ISBN 978-1-934389-46-1

POSTMODERNISM FOR BEGINNERS: ISBN 978-1-934389-09-6

RELATIVITY & QUANTUM PHYSICS FOR BEGINNERS: ISBN 978-1-934389-42-3

SARTRE FOR BEGINNERS: ISBN 978-1-934389-15-7

SHAKESPEARE FOR BEGINNERS: ISBN 978-1-934389-29-4

STRUCTURALISM & POSTSTRUCTURALISM FOR BEGINNERS: ISBN 978-1-934389-10-2

WOMEN'S HISTORY FOR BEGINNERS: ISBN 978-1-934389-60-7

UNIONS FOR BEGINNERS: ISBN 978-1-934389-77-5

U.S. CONSTITUTION FOR BEGINNERS: ISBN 978-1-934389-62-1

ZEN FOR BEGINNERS: ISBN 978-1-934389-06-5

ZINN FOR BEGINNERS: ISBN 978-1-934389-40-9

www.forbeginnersbooks.com